Unbreak My Heart

Unbreak My Heart

A MEMOIR

TONI BRAXTON

Some names have been changed where indicated in order to protect the privacy of individuals involved.

Photographs courtesy of the author unless otherwise noted.

HarperCollins books may be purchased for educational, business, or sales promotional use. For information please e-mail the Special Markets department at SPsales@harpercollins.com.

FIRST EDITION

Designed by Paula Russell Szafranski

Library of Congress Cataloging-in-Publication Data has been applied for.

ISBN 978-0-06-229328-2

14 15 16 17 18   OV/RRD   10 9 8 7 6 5 4 3 2 1

*To Denim and Diezel—the two gifts who
will forever make my heart whole*

CONTENTS

Contents

INTRODUCTION

I'm at a crossroads. More than four decades ago, I set out on a journey as a little girl with a huge dream—one that has carried me all the way from a dirt-filled plot in Severn, Maryland, to the stage of the Grammys and beyond. In one way, it's a phenomenal gift to have your wildest dream actually come true. But in another way, when that happens, it can leave you with a profound sense of uncertainty about what to do next. That's the juncture at which I stand—right in the middle of creating a road map of what my life could look like tomorrow. Next year. In a decade. Forever.

My dream is as much born of passion as it is of deep reflection—that is the privilege of carving out a new path in adulthood, during life's second act. This book is the sum total of that reflection. On every page, in every sentence, with every anecdote I recount, I am daring to examine both the steps and missteps that have led me to this moment. But I'm not simply looking back as some kind of emotional exercise—for me, the point is to find my way to the next best place.

Someone wise once said that pain is information—it's our bodies' way of telling us, "Pay attention—something isn't working here." So especially as I ponder the most distressing moments of my journey—those times when life has become burdensome enough to take me to the brink—I'm looking ahead with that ultimate hope. And what is that hope? That peering back at my past heartbreaks will ultimately lead to healing. That is the only real point in reflecting on any experience—to find a purpose in it that leads you toward wholeness.

Nothing about my story and yours may seem to resemble each other at first glance. And yes, it's true—my mountaintop moments and my lowest points really are unique to me. Only I can tell you what it's like to live through the combination of experiences that has filled my years. But from another perspective, my path is also very much like the one you've traveled. You may not have grown up as the first-born of six in a town few people have even heard of. You may not have been diagnosed with lupus, cared for a son with autism, or cried your way through two humiliating bankruptcies and an agonizing divorce. But like every other person who has ever lived, you know what it means to ache. To love. To laugh. To regret. Our circumstances may be different—but the emotions that come with being human are what connect us all.

The lessons of my journey are plentiful—and here is one. I've realized just how much of myself I've suppressed. I've sacrificed a lot of who I am to make the people around me happy. No longer. I've entrusted people who didn't have my best interest at heart. That chapter is now permanently closed. I don't know exactly what the coming years will bring, but I do know this: I will never again hand over my power to another human being. To do so is to hand over life itself—and at long last, I'm getting mine back.

You may know me best by the songs I've shared with the world. "Breathe Again." "Seven Whole Days." "Un-break My Heart." To know my creations is to indeed know one part of who I am. But behind every lyric, behind each of those melodies and countless others, there lies a story that I've never been brave enough to tell. In this moment—standing at this crossroads—I have at last found the courage.

CHAPTER 1

Losing My Breath

The happiest day of my career arrived one February morning in 1991. Nothing could have prepared me for how that day would end.

"Hey, what are you doing?" I immediately recognized the voice on the phone as that of Greg, my then-manager.

"Not much," I lied, since I'd been pacing the carpeted floor of the town house I shared with a roommate in Laurel, Maryland. At the time, I was a student at Bowie State University, which is now the University of Maryland at Bowie. "What's up?" I tightened my grip on the receiver and pressed it to my right ear. Even before he could answer, I somehow knew my life was about to shift. The only surprise would be how.

Since years before that phone call, I'd always dreamed I'd be a famous singer. My mother, Evelyn—who once turned down a music scholarship so she could marry my father, Michael—filled our Maryland home with music. "Joshua fought the Battle of Jericho and the walls came tumblin' down," Mommy would belt out in an operatic style when I was just a toddler. With so much music in the air, I and my five younger siblings—Mikey, Traci, Towanda, Trina, and Tamar—learned to harmonize practically before we learned to speak. And since we spent nearly as much time in church as we did at home (my father eventually became a pastor), we were surrounded by the rich and soulful tunes my parents passed on to us. Mommy eventually recognized our potential and turned my sisters and me into the Braxtons, a quintet-style singing group. That was just the beginning.

On weekends and after school under Mommy's strict guidance, the five of us rehearsed for hours in churches around town. Each time we performed—usually right after my father had delivered a riveting sermon to a packed house—we heard a familiar refrain: "Them Braxton girls sure can sing!" All that practicing eventually paid off: In 1989, we signed a deal with Arista Records, and a year later, we put out our first single, "Good Life." The song wasn't exactly a hit (it reached number 79 on the *Billboard* Hot Black Singles chart), but we were still over the moon. Not so for Arista.

Though Clive Davis and the other record execs recognized that we had talent, no one quite knew how to package a group of squeaky-clean sisters who ranged from a twenty-three-year-old with a contralto voice (me) all the way down to a thirteen-year-old who still wore braces (Tamar). So after our lukewarm debut, Clive handed us off to a songwriting and production duo that had just formed a label under Arista. That's right: Kenneth "Babyface" Edmonds and Antonio "L.A." Reid invited us to fly to Atlanta and put on a showcase audition. We were elated.

How exactly do you prepare for such a make-or-break moment? My sisters and I did it by practicing like crazy. Every day for a month, I drove from my place in Laurel to my parents' home in Severn so we could rehearse. I put together a medley that included harmonies from the Carpenters' song "Close to You"; our first single, "Good Life"; and Janet Jackson's hit "Love Will Never Do (Without You)." Throughout the performance, each one of us had a solo—mine was "God Is," a gospel song. We sang a cappella for some of the pieces and I played the keyboard for others. My solo was to be the final one of the showcase.

In between our marathon rehearsals, I shopped for our stage outfits—as the eldest, I was in charge of that. So I drove over to Lerner's (the store that carried plenty of extra-smalls!) and picked out black stirrup pants and leggings for the girls and a pair of keyhole earrings for each of us. Traci got the cutest outfit: a black one-piece catsuit along with a matching black jacket that had gold trim on it—very Salt-n-Pepa. As the shorty in the group (I was barely five foot one), I had to find some way to stand out. That's why I chose a special outfit for myself: white biker shorts with lace trim, a belt with a silver buckle, a white jacket with long sleeves, and suede boots that I wore scrunched down—very 1980s Madonna. Mommy and Dad also bought each of us a black leather Kool Moe Dee–ish trench coat. A couple days later, we flew off from our home in Maryland and toward the kind of opportunity you only get once.

The night before the audition, my sisters and I; our parents; our manager, Greg; and Vernon Slaughter, then vice president of LaFace Records, spread out across six rooms at the Hilton Garden Inn on Peachtree Street. When the bellhop took our suitcases, I offered him a tip. Though the continental breakfast and coffee were free, I also proudly left a few crumpled dollar bills for the waiter. I felt so grown-up—like a star on an episode of *Dynasty*.

The following morning, a driver picked us up from the hotel in a white, extra-long stretch limo and dropped us off at an empty, dimly lit club on Piedmont Road. We arrived at exactly two P.M. And we waited. And we sweated. And we squirmed. When L.A. and Kenny finally strode in around two forty-five, each of us stood up, shyly greeted the two of them, and filed onto the stage. We then took our places and launched right into our opening song, "Good Life." The lights were so bright that I could hardly see their faces—which is probably good because the butterflies were already swarming in my stomach.

Yet our jitters didn't stop us from delivering a great show. All those years of church performances kicked in, and we nailed every one of the songs. By the time I took the keyboard for my solo, my anxiousness had given way to confidence.

"She can really play," Kenny leaned over and said to L.A., who may have thought I was faking it during the other numbers; by the way I was holding my hands, Kenny could tell I was a real pianist.

After our audition, L.A. and Kenny walked up to the stage and chatted with us. "Anybody else here play an instrument?" asked L.A.

"Traci plays the drums," I blurted out.

"She plays the drums?" he said.

I suddenly remembered that L.A. had been a star drummer in the Deele, an R&B band. My throat tightened. "Well, she kinda plays the church drums," I explained.

"Oh, okay," he said—but then he didn't ask her to show him. Years later, I'd wonder whether I'd robbed Traci of her big moment by minimizing her drum skills.

"We were impressed with you guys," L.A. finally said.

"You were great," Kenny added.

Really? I thought. *Could that be true?* A moment later, we walked off the stage, put on our matching trenches, and waited for nearly an hour while Greg and our parents talked with L.A. and Kenny. On the limo ride back to the hotel, Greg gave us a reason to feel hopeful. "They really liked you guys!" he said. "I think they're going to sign you." Whatever happened, I knew we'd given our best.

Back in Maryland, we told every person we knew about our audition. "What was Babyface like?" a friend asked me.

"He was the *nicest* guy," I cooed. "And actually, I've met him twice—I once talked to him backstage on *Soul Train.*"

In 1998, I took a cross-country trip to Los Angeles and went to *Soul Train*. As the following two weeks snaked along and I awaited word from L.A. and Kenny through my manager, I could hardly contain my excitement. Every morning, I called Greg and said, "Have you heard anything?" He hadn't. So on the morning when Greg actually did call me, my eagerness had already reached level 10.

"So I have some good news for you," he said with hardly a pause between each word. "L.A. and Kenny thought you guys were great." I froze. As that statement was sinking in, Greg followed it with another. "But I also have some bad news," he said, continuing. "They don't want to sign your sisters." I stopped breathing for a moment. *Did I hear him wrong?*

"Um, what do you mean?" I said once I'd recovered.

"They're about to sign another girl group," Greg explained. "And quite honestly, they don't know what to do with you and your sisters because your age differences are so extreme. They acknowledge that all of you can sing, but . . ."

Long pause.

"L.A. and Kenny only want you."

"Well," I finally said, with hot blood racing through my veins, "I'm not going to do it if they don't sign all of us. Let me talk to my mother about it."

"Toni, I wouldn't do that if I were you," Greg said, lowering his voice by a full octave. "Let's just sort through this and come up with a plan before we present it to your mom, okay?"

"No, no, no—I'm going to call Mommy," I shot back. "She'll know what to do. I'll let you know and call you later."

"You can't say no to L.A. and Kenny—they can sign any artist they want!" said Greg. "You're so close now, Toni. Don't let this pass you by."

I knew my mother would have the best answer—especially in light of a story she often told us. "When I was much younger," she'd say, "I was in a singing group, the Viewettes. A rep from Motown wanted to sign only me, but I turned it down. There's no telling where my life would be today if I had taken that deal." So that evening, I picked up the phone to call the one woman I trusted more than any other in the world.

"They loved the showcase, Mommy," I began. I paused. "But they don't want to sign the other girls. They just want me."

Total silence.

"Did you hear me, Mommy?"

"I heard you," she said sternly. "So what are you going to do, Toni?"

"I don't really know what I'm going to do," I said, shrugging. "I'm just talking to you about it." I wanted to remind her that she was once in the same situation when she was a young girl in a singing group.

"Well it sounds like you've already made up your mind!" Mom cut in. I told her I'd be over to talk to the girls about it.

My brain shifted into overdrive. *What just happened?* I thought. *What did I say wrong? Why was my mother so upset?* Immediately, I called my brother, Mikey, at my parents' home and recounted the scene. "You've gotta do what's best for you, Toni," said Mikey, who was always the levelheaded one.

"You're never gonna get another chance like this." I thanked him for his encouragement and then we hung up. Less than an hour later, he called again.

"Toni, you'd better come to the house right now."

"What do you mean?" I said, my heartbeat quickening.

"Mommy is talking to the girls," he said. "Just get over here fast."

A half hour later, I came through the back door of my parents' home; Mommy passed me in the kitchen and didn't speak. The energy was so thick you could cut it. I darted into Mikey's room and sat down. "So what's going on?" I asked, pressing him. What my brother revealed still makes me shudder.

Right after I'd called my mother that evening with the news from Greg, said Mikey, Mommy had gathered the girls. " 'You're about to hear something that's going to vex you to your soul,' " she told them. " 'The devil is raging, and we've gotta bind that enemy.' " As Mikey told me the story, I stared at him in disbelief.

Once I'd regained my composure, I wandered through the house and asked each one of the girls to join me in the living room. Mommy sat off to the side with her arms folded. My dad joined her—and he had the same tense energy.

"Why don't you tell your sisters what you told me?" she spat. I stood before them for what felt like an eternity before I uttered my first syllable. "Um, L.A. and Kenny really liked all of us," I said. I stopped to inhale before I delivered part two. "But," I mumbled, "they only want to sign me." All at once, the room erupted with a sound that I hope to never hear again—all four of my sisters sobbed as they cupped their faces in their hands. Finally, after a full two minutes of bawling, Traci looked up at me. "Toni, maybe you can sign and then come back and get us after you make a name for yourself," she said. I nodded and promised to do so. I hugged and kissed each of my sisters, and I tried to kiss my parents—but they turned away. So I then left the room, and drove home in tears.

Once at home, I sat in my apartment and stared into space. Years later, I would begin to understand my mother's reaction—but on that evening in February, I didn't at all see it coming. Yes, my parents have always been tough, yet I would've never anticipated that they would be so angry at me. As the sun descended on the best and worst day of my life, I had never felt more confused. *Maybe Mikey and Traci are right,* I thought. *Maybe I should just take the deal.* After rehearsing the episode over and over again in my head, I cried myself to sleep.

At ten the next morning, I finally called Greg.

"How did it go with your mother?" he asked.

"Not good," I said.

"I told you it wasn't going to be good, Toni," he said. "So what are you going to do now?"

I drew in a breath. "I'm going to sign," I finally said.

That was the beginning of my guilt. In the coming years, I did everything I could to help my sisters get their big break. I took them along with me to events and award shows. I hired them to be my background singers. I introduced them to other artists and music execs. I even helped them secure their own record deal on LaFace records. Yet in spite of how much I invested, they never experienced the same level of fame that I did. So I carried that weight through every part of my career. Through six Grammy Awards. Through sixty million records sold around the world. Through two humiliating bankruptcies, a heart-wrenching divorce, and an illness that still threatens my life. And at every major milestone along my path, my mother's admonition echoed in the background: "Don't forget your sisters."

I didn't. In fact, since the day Mommy made it clear that my success was to always be split five ways, I've fought to be sure that my sisters could share their voices. What I didn't expect is that I'd somehow lose my own.

Until now.

My answer was yes to the solo deal—but it was the saddest yes I've ever given. Exactly one week after I signed, I traded the only home I'd known for an unfamiliar world just over the horizon. What I'd discover during my journey would change me forever.

CHAPTER 2

Country Life in the Suburbs

My mother, Evelyn, was barely thirteen when her own mom sent her off to a new world. "You're going to stay with your aunt Juanita in Severn," my grandmother Beulah Jackson told her. Juanita—Beulah's sister—had tried for many years to have children with her husband, Roland, but the couple was infertile. So in the summer of 1962, when Aunt Juanita drove down to visit her sister in Cayce, South Carolina, the two made an agreement: My aunt would take one of Beulah's nine children back to Severn to raise. My mother—who was the second youngest among her siblings—was that child.

Mommy actually wanted to go. You'd think she would've been reluctant to leave her family and live in a different state— but she was eager to experience some freedom. Aunt Juanita had always been particularly fond of my mother, so it wasn't all that surprising that she chose her to adopt. "You're so lucky," said Mommy's sister Vernaree, who'd wanted to be picked. Earthaleen, who, unlike my mother, had actually visited Aunt Juanita in Severn, seemed unimpressed. "It was just okay," she told Mommy when she returned from a trip there. But Aunt Juanita described her home so beautifully: "There's a big house and a white picket fence, with red roses cascading all around it," she said. Mommy couldn't wait.

When my mother showed up on Queenstown Road in Severn, the "big house" turned out to be a small trailer. Aunt Juanita and Uncle Roland (I called him "Ro Ro") had inherited a few acres from my uncle's family right after they married, and on that land, they lived in a two-bedroom trailer; Mommy moved into their second bedroom. Though the surrounding neighborhood was mostly filled with Caucasians, all of Queenstown Road was owned by traditional African-American families—and many of those families were somehow related to each other. Like my family, a lot of them had moved to Maryland from down south. When they showed up in Severn, they brought part of their Southern lifestyle with them—the traditions of canning and pickling, the backyard gardens filled with collards and tomatoes, and of course, the soul food cooking. The residents on Queenstown Road were neither urban nor rural—they were what I call "country suburban."

Once Mommy moved to Severn as the new girl in the neighborhood, Aunt Juanita encouraged her to be social. So my mother quickly made friends and joined her school choir.

Mommy absolutely loved to sing, and in those days, opera was considered the proper music. Around the trailer, Aunt Juanita would often hear Mommy singing, opera style, the Motown and gospel songs she loved. Mommy was and still is a gifted vocalist, and she was chosen to be part of the Maryland state choir. Mommy also formed a singing group called the Viewettes, along with her friends Mary, Almeda, and Valorie. They won a few competitions and trophies.

Within months of moving to Severn, Mom's social life had fully blossomed. One evening, my mother asked my aunt to let her attend an annual dance at the YMCA. "Aunt Juanita, can I go to the dance?" Mom asked.

"When is it?"

"It's tonight."

Aunt Juanita paused. "You can go," she finally said. Mom dashed right to her bedroom, slipped on her prettiest outfit, and dashed off from the trailer. She met up with her two best friends, Almeda and Juanita (yes, there were a lot of Juanitas back then . . .). The three of them showed up at the YMCA together.

That night, a fifteen-year-old young man from Baltimore spotted my mother on the dance floor. Mommy pretended not to notice as he meandered toward her. "Would you like to dance?" the boy asked.

"I don't really feel like dancing," said Mommy, who wasn't attracted to him.

"What's your name?" he asked.

"I'm Joan," Mom fibbed. But throughout the event, several of Mom's friends blew her cover when they yelled out her nickname: "Hey, Ev!"

Later, the young man made a second attempt to capture Mommy's attention. "I thought your name was Joan," he said, grinning. "So why is everyone calling you Evelyn?" he asked.

"My friends call me that," Mommy admitted, blushing a little.

"Well," he said, "I'll call you that, too." That's how my mother met Michael Conrad Braxton Sr.—my father.

Race played a role in the arrival of my father's family to Maryland. Dad's mom, Eva, was nearly 90 percent Caucasian, yet she was still considered black in this country, thanks to the one-drop rule. Grandma Eva was born in New York, but when her extended family discovered she was partly black, her mother sent her down to Calvert County, Maryland, to be raised by one of her relatives. Eva looked as white as Edith Bunker in *All in the Family,* yet because she was biracial, she didn't really fit in anywhere. When the teachers at her boarding school realized she was partly African American, they dipped her strawberry-blond hair into tea to make it darker, then braided her dark strands into plaits to signal her ethnic heritage. After Grandma Eva endured that painful childhood and grew into a young woman, she eventually met my grandfather, Frances Braxton—a descendant of Carter Braxton, the Virginia delegate who signed the Declaration of Independence in 1776. My grandfather Frances, who was half African-American and half Native American, had a dark beautiful skin tone. In part, Eva chose Frances as her husband because he was so dark—she didn't want her own children to grow up with any questions or confusion about their racial identity. My father, Michael, was Frances and Eva's second child and first son.

Fast-forward to that YMCA dance—which was the night Daddy fell for Mommy from the moment he first saw her. In the months to follow, my father would either hitchhike or take the bus to travel the sixteen miles from his Baltimore home to Mommy's trailer in Severn. Aunt Juanita liked Michael right away, but she wasn't all that pleased that Mommy was starting to date—my mother was still pretty young. Of course, back in those days, "dating" usually meant dropping by to sit in the living room and watch television while the grown-ups sat right there in between you! There wasn't much trouble they could get into.

After weeks of talking on the phone, they went on their first date outside the house. My dad took my mother out for dinner and a movie. Afterward, he brought her back to the front door of Aunt Juanita's trailer and gently kissed her on the lips. They said good night and Mommy slipped inside. A second later, Mom heard a knock. It was my father—and he stood there holding her wig in his right hand! The Dorothy Dandridge–style wig had somehow slipped off my mother's head while they were kissing. When Mommy spotted her wig in Dad's hand and realized he was staring right at the stocking cap on her head, she let out a scream, grabbed the wig before Dad had a chance to say anything, and then slammed the door. That must've been a real good kiss!

Before my mother even finished high school, she and the other girls in her singing group caught the ear of a Motown rep. The rep offered to sign only my mother, but she blew that opportunity because she refused to leave the group. By then, Mommy already had her heart set on another passion—marriage.

Soon after my mother's seventeenth birthday in 1966, my father traveled down to South Carolina to get my grandfather's permission to marry his daughter—in Maryland, you need parental consent to marry when you're under eighteen. My mother was eager to take her vows so she could get out of Aunt Juanita's house. She loved her aunt, of course, but she sometimes felt that Juanita was possessive. Mommy once even wrote a letter to her mother and asked if she could return to South Carolina; she sealed the envelope and gave it to Aunt Juanita to mail for her. Months later, Mommy found the unsealed letter in her aunt's room. She had never sent it. A few years later, we all discovered one reason my aunt might've held on so tightly to my mother: Juanita had realized that her husband was having an affair.

Back when my uncle was a young man in Severn, he had a hometown sweetheart. He eventually joined the army and left for a post in Arizona—and while he was there, he fell in love with my aunt Juanita. My aunt got pregnant, so my uncle married her. My aunt lost that child, and over time, my uncle began cheating with his first love. In 1970, Uncle Ro Ro was on top of his mistress—and right then and there, he died of a heart attack.

At the time, I was too young to even know what sex was. Yet when I overheard my mother telling that story, I became paranoid that the same thing could one day happen to me.

When my father made his way down to South Carolina to ask for my mother's hand in marriage, my grandfather—the Reverend John Jacob Jackson Jr.—gave his blessing. A few months later at the Metropolitan United Methodist Church at the end of Queenstown Road, my parents had a "rainbow wedding"—Mom's bridesmaids wore a variety of colors, like red, blue, and sea-breeze green. But my parents don't have any pictures from their wedding day: The film got ruined, or at least that's the story they told me. So a few weeks after the wedding, Mom put back on her dress, Dad put back on his suit, and they posed for a photo with Aunt Juanita and Uncle Roland. After the marriage, my aunt and uncle gave my parents two acres of their land, and Mommy and Daddy put a trailer on the plot.

On October 7, 1967—less than a year into their marriage—my parents brought me home from the hospital and settled me into our white, two-bedroom trailer with the turquoise shutters. I've often wondered why Mommy gave up her chance at a singing career to become a wife and mother—and because my mother is still so guarded about her childhood, I may never know the reason. But in a way, I'm here today because she made that choice.

. . .

I ADORED MY aunt Juanita. As a toddler, I couldn't quite pronounce her name, so she let me call her Nita. Especially since I was Mommy's first child, my aunt spoiled me. "Pick out anything you want," she'd tell me whenever we'd stop at Woolworth's, the five-and-dime store. We were usually on our way back from Johns Hopkins in Baltimore—by the time I was five, my parents had discovered that I had the trait for glaucoma. So each time I returned to the hospital for a follow-up exam, I had to have my pupils dilated—and that meant I needed sunglasses until my eyesight returned to normal. "How about these?" Nita would say, holding up a pair of seventies psychedelic shades with sparkles on the rims. I nodded yes. We'd sometimes leave the store with a couple pair of glasses, plus a bag filled with candy and bubble gum for the road. At times, Nita felt more like my grandmother than my great-aunt—especially since she'd adopted Mommy. Even once my other siblings came along, I was still my aunt's favorite.

I'll always remember the day Mommy brought home my little brother, Mikey. My grandma Eva, who lived in Baltimore, had a reddish-orange tabby cat named Snowball; Grandma probably had a white cat at some point, and after she lost it, she named every new cat Snowball. To me, Mikey looked just like the Tabby cat. My brother was tiny and pale, with red hair and greenish eyes that he likely inherited from my white grandmother. "Mommy, the cat is crying," I'd say when Mikey let out a whimper from his crib. Though my brother was odd looking, he was the most adorable little brother I could've asked for.

As Mikey and I grew up, we both always looked forward to visiting our maternal grandmother, Beulah Jackson. Dad would drive our family from Severn to our grandparents' home in Cayce, South Carolina. We usually pulled out of our driveway at two in the morning while it was still dark so that we could avoid traffic. When the sun was finally up, I'd awaken in the backseat of our sand-colored convertible Bonneville and start asking my parents, "Are we there yet?" The trip was only about eight hours—but when I was small, it felt more like eighty-eight hours.

Mommy would keep my brother and me occupied with toys and a coloring book in the backseat. Somewhere along the route, we'd usually stop at KFC and buy a bucket of original recipe chicken (no baked back then!). I knew we were nearly at Grandma's place once we reached a certain landmark we always stopped at—a roadside attraction called South of the Border, which is located between Dillon, South Carolina, and Rowland, North Carolina. The rest stop's mascot was Pedro, a Mexican bandito dressed in a poncho and sombrero. From there, we only had about two more hours to go.

At the rest stop, Mommy would call Grandma from the pay phone and let her know what time we'd arrive. Long before we even pulled into her driveway, my grandmother would sit in her rocking chair on the front porch and await the first glimpse of our car; Grandpa would sit alongside her, chewing tobacco and spitting it into a blue Maxwell House coffee can. For hours, they would sway back and forth and wave as friends and neighbors passed. My grandparents lived in the kind of neighborhood where everyone knew everyone else; in their little suburban town, most of the modest rancher houses came with a porch and a small yard enclosed by a wooden picket fence. "Hey dere!" Grandma would call out whenever she spotted someone on the sidewalk out front. That's just the kind of thing traditional country Southern folk did—sit, wave, rock, and wait.

As soon as we rounded the corner onto her street, Grandma's eyes lit up. "Hey, ya'll!" she'd call out, welcoming us from the stairs of the porch. Once we pulled into the driveway, my brother and I nearly leapt out of the car because we were so tired of sitting. "Hi, Grandma!" we'd scream, running toward her. She'd sweep Mikey and me into a warm embrace and squeeze us so tightly. "Come here!" she'd say. "Grandma needs her sugar!" Even from the front driveway, I could smell what she had on for supper: yellow rice, biscuits, hog maws, and fried chicken.

Before we entered the front door of the four-bedroom house, we had to unpack the car—which was a job that I absolutely hated doing. My parents had loaded suitcases and bags into every part of our Bonneville: in the trunk, in the backseat, even on top. When Mikey and I were little, Mommy would take us straight inside—but when we got old enough to help, my brother and I had to drag in each of the bags, one at a time, as my parents unloaded them.

Later, our efforts were richly rewarded: Grandma Beulah always served us a slice of the most delicious homemade pound cake I've ever tasted. Grandma's friend, a lady across the street, had baked the cake—she was known around the neighborhood as one of the best bakers in the Carolinas. Everyone called the lady Miss Red Dress, which puzzled me. "How come they call her Miss Red Dress?" I once asked Mommy. "Because one day, she wore a red dress," Mommy explained, "and Lawd, she must've been *wearing* that red dress 'cause the name stuck!" Whenever Mommy told us a story, she acted as if she was narrating a commercial for the United Negro College Fund.

All of us kids spent a lot of time in the backyard—we weren't allowed to play in the main sitting room because we might break something. Out back, an old rusted well sat in one corner of the yard, and though it worked, my grandparents didn't use it. A clothesline drooped across half the yard; whenever Grandma brought in dried bedsheets and made up our bed, the sheets smelled like a mix of earth and chickens. Yes, that's right: My grandparents kept a gaggle of chickens and one rooster. I used to hate seeing the rooster pounce on top of the chickens and bully them—at the time, I had no idea that the rooster's aggressiveness is what produced so many eggs for my grandparents.

Grandma also kept a small garden in her backyard. Tomatoes, collards, string beans, a little corn—you name it, and you could find it in Grandma's garden. Both at Grandma's house and at our home in Severn, we ate well. Our dinner table typically overflowed with fresh vegetables, smothered chicken, baked yams, and buttermilk biscuits with strawberry preserves that we'd canned ourselves. When Mommy was a girl, Grandma taught her how to preserve everything from watermelon rinds and jam to cucumbers and peaches. Though my grandparents and parents were working-class people, one thing is for certain: We ate like royalty.

Indoors, my grandparents' furniture was covered with plastic—that's how old folks used to preserve their sofas. I hated to fall asleep on the couch; my face would sweat and stick to the plastic. Underneath the covering, Grandma's velour couch had been reupholstered many times since she purchased it in the late 1920s; the sofa's golden-colored fabric had tones of dark royal purple. The rest of the living room was like a museum celebrating our extended family: Grandma's fireplace was flanked with old photos of aunts, uncles, and cousins I'd never met.

Some had on caps and gowns; others wore military uniforms. "Who's that?" I once asked Grandma, pointing at a face I didn't recognize. "Baby, that's your cousin!" she said, laughing. The man in the photo looked older than my mother, so I thought he must be my uncle. But since my mother is one of the youngest of her nine siblings (Grandma Beulah was forty-two when she had Mommy!), some of my mother's older siblings have children who are older than Mommy.

After supper, our whole family would gather 'round an old upright piano and sing. Aunt Vernaree, Aunt Earthaleen, Aunt Loretta, and Aunt Hattie—four of my mother's sisters—

lived within a minute by foot of Grandma Beulah. Each time we came to town, we'd always start out at my grandparents' house before dispersing to my aunts' homes. My uncle, who lived fifteen minutes away by car, usually drove over to join us. All of my aunts had pianos; once we'd assembled, one of my aunts or cousins would start out by singing an old Negro spiritual in a low minor key. Later, they'd transition to a jubilant church song. "Oh happy day!" my older cousin Brenda— Aunt Hattie's daughter—would belt out in her thunderous voice. "Oh happy day!" By the end of the song, all of us were on our feet, clapping along and chiming in. Afterward, someone would say, "Lawd, that Brenda sure can sing!" I couldn't wait to grow up and become one of the main singers.

At bedtime, my whole family retired to my grandparents' back room, which was right off the kitchen. In that gigantic room, Grandma kept two of the hugest king-sized four-poster beds I'd ever seen. In fact, the beds were so big that my siblings and I could share one of them; Mom and Dad took the other. To this day, I still love four-poster beds.

Just before we left town, Dad would drive us over to a local produce stand so we could pick out watermelons, cantaloupes, wild bullet grapes, and green tomatoes—the tomatoes had to be green in order to make it all the way back up north; afterward, we'd all return to the house so my grandparents could see us off. Grandma always sent us back to Maryland with a round of hugs, a lot of love, and plenty of fresh collards from her garden. "Y'all drive safely!" she'd yell toward us as Dad slowly backed out of the driveway. "And call me when you get home!" She'd then stand there on the porch and watch after us down the road until the rear end of our Bonneville disappeared.

Every summer and at least three times a year during my childhood, we made the trip to South Carolina. Most of the time the journey was filled with laughter, music, and celebration—but I do remember one year when the energy was somber. Aunt Vernaree's daughter, my older cousin Lisa, died when she was seven. She and some other kids went swimming in a pond and Lisa drowned. Aunt Vernaree rushed over to the pond at exactly the wrong moment: the arm of the tractor that had raked the pond held Lisa's lifeless body up in the air. I don't think my aunt ever fully recovered from the heart-ache, and our whole family felt deeply saddened by the loss. "Don't bother your aunt right now," Mommy kept telling me and Mikey during that trip. "Her nerves are bad." For a while, that changed the spirit and energy of our trips. But over time, the joy slowly returned.

Each time we arrived home to Severn, our lives quickly settled back into a familiar rhythm. My father arose at six each morning to get ready for his job. Daddy worked as the display manager at Korvettes, a discount department store that was the Target of the seventies. Dad's store was on Ritchie Highway in Glen Burnie, Maryland. For most of my childhood, Mommy stayed home with us; when she and Dad first married, she'd worked as a candy striper at the University of Maryland, but she gave that up to become a full-time homemaker. So every morning, she awakened just as early as Dad did, made her way into our kitchen, and prepared my father's breakfast—usually an egg sandwich, which was her version of an Egg McMuffin. Once Dad had swallowed his final swig of coffee, he headed toward the front door of our trailer, sometimes with his half-eaten sandwich still in hand. I'd often stumble, sleepy eyed, from my bedroom and catch my parents pecking each other on the lips to say good-bye.

LOVE, FAMILY, FAITH, tradition—those Southern values filled every part of my earliest memories in Severn. We relied on God. We shared our lives with each other, with our friends and relatives, and with the neighbors who lived alongside us. And above all else, we built a rock-solid family foundation—one that would soon be tested.

CHAPTER 3

Pillar of Deceit

My family was always religious—but the year I was seven, they became even more religious. "From now on," Mommy told me one morning, "you're going to be wearing dresses. The Bible says a woman should not wear anything pertaining to a man." At our new church, Pillar of Truth, this was the strict rule—one of many I'd soon discover.

For a full year before we joined that Apostolic Pentecostal congregation, my parents had been on a spiritual search. My mother, who was raised Baptist, and my father, who grew up United Methodist, never told me what prompted their exploration—but I think it was a spiritual hunger.

Around that time, my family moved from our trailer to a newly constructed three-bedroom town house in another part of Severn. Months before the move, my parents got to pick out the interiors—a red shag carpet, a red and black fireplace, a washer and dryer off the kitchen, a backyard, and sidewalks out front; Dad said I'd be able to ride my bike.

"We're even going to have a foyer," Mommy told me.

"What's a foyer?" I asked.

"It's a section at the front of the house before you go into the living room," she explained. As it turned out, the "foyer" was really the tiniest linoleum-lined area right at the front door—but that didn't make me any less excited about our new home. I didn't know it then, but I'd experience some of the pivotal moments of my girlhood in that house.

Once we moved into that neighborhood, what was happening there certainly encouraged my parents' spiritual quest. We got used to hearing a knock at our front door and opening it to find a Muslim, a Jehovah's Witness, or even an Avon rep; during the seventies, it seemed like everyone was passing out religious pamphlets, salesman style. On weekends, our family began visiting all different kinds of services, from Catholic to Muslim. The Muslim guy who sold bean pies to my parents stopped by our house often; the three of them would get into long, intellectual conversations in our living room. A similar thing happened when my parents considered becoming Jehovah's Witnesses—people were constantly dropping in to talk with my parents about crosses and constellations. In the winter of 1974, my parents finally chose Pillar of Truth as our church home. That choice would have lasting consequences for all of us.

Bishop Scurry, our church's leader, was an attractive, heavyset, fair-skinned black woman who was probably in her midsixties. Her husband had a limp because one of his legs was shorter than the other. Through my seven-year-old eyes, the bishop seemed like a grandmother—she had a calm and nurturing presence, and she wore gold metal-framed glasses and a white hat affixed to her head by a black bobby pin on each side. And she led a church with very strict rules.

As members of the church, in addition to wearing only skirts or dresses, the women and girls had to "cover their nakedness" by placing a hat over at least 75 percent of their heads. Every Sunday, the church ladies would show up in hats that looked like the kind Elijah Muhammad wore, minus the tassel; the men wore gentlemen's caps. According to Bishop Scurry's interpretation of the Old Testament, it was a sin to bare too much of the body, including the arms and the legs above the knees. In fact, my mother stitched extra fabric onto her hemlines so that they'd fall below her knee. And here's the part that really doesn't make sense: Ankle-length formal dresses were banned.

Even during the muggy summer months, all the women wore full stockings. A watch was the only piece of jewelry allowed. Makeup was completely prohibited. If you disobeyed any of the rules, you were completely ostracized. And if the rapture came while you were in this phase, you wouldn't make it to heaven.

Did I mention several of my family members thought that my parents were crazy? Once when my aunt Earthaleen came to visit us, she and Mommy got into it. "Ain't you tired of wearing all these dresses?" she snapped. She and Aunt Nita couldn't believe that my parents would get involved in this kind of church—one that didn't even allow us to celebrate Christmas or put up a tree. During our first year at the church, my older cousin Kimmy, then ten, came to live with us for a few years until her own family could sort out some issues—but she sometimes still went home on the weekends to be with her mom. I felt jealous that Kim got to wear pants and listen to secular music.

During our first Christmas at Pillar of Truth, I really wanted a Baby Alive, a battery-operated doll that I could feed. "I can't get it for you, Toni," my aunt told me. "Your mother is going to be upset." Even still, I begged Mommy to let Aunt Juanita get me the doll. "We don't celebrate no *darn* Christmas," said Mommy, who often used the word *darn* to keep from cursing. In fact, we didn't acknowledge most holidays in our church—no Thanksgiving, no Easter, and especially no Halloween. According to the bishop, these were pagan holidays. Even still, I prayed very hard for my doll—and I felt so guilty that I did.

You may find this hard to believe, but I was excited the first time Mommy told me I could only wear dresses. By first grade, I'd already become a girly girl—pink and lavender were my two favorite colors, and my closet was filled with frilly pieces. Before school, Mommy would lay out the dress she'd selected for me, along with a pair of ruffle socks and black and white oxfords from Kinney shoes. Yet after months of sashaying around like an African-American version of Shirley Temple, the day arrived when I craved something different. I wanted to wear pants.

One morning, I spotted the taupe dress with a navy blue vertical stripe in the center that my mother had placed on the red chair in our upstairs foyer. A moment later, I dashed to my bedroom to dig out an outfit I'd tucked away—a pair of chocolate corduroys and a soft pink sweater.

"You have to wear a dress," Mommy said when she noticed the corduroys I'd pulled out.

"But why, Mommy?" I protested.

"Because dresses are for girls and pants are for boys," she said. That was the only explanation I received.

We practically lived at church. Once we entered the brick building that had the steepest cement stairs I'd ever climbed, the service would go on forever. After Sunday school at nine A.M., the main service at eleven carried on until the last tambourine had gone silent, which was usually around two P.M. Afterward, the members gathered for a meal. The church leaders sold plates of fried chicken, potato salad, and collard greens for $1.50 each, and lemon cake with chocolate icing, which I still call "church cake." The proceeds went to the building improvement fund or to the sick and shut-in fund. As our family grew and Dad's budget tightened, we'd often leave the church and drive to the supermarket to purchase our own lunch—baloney, mayo, and cheese on white bread. "Don't make a mess back there," Mommy would warn Kimmy, Mikey, and me from the front seat of our Bonneville.

In the middle row of the backseat, I balanced a paper towel on my lap to catch the crumbs. Our day didn't end there: After lunch, we returned for an afternoon program at four, followed by evening service at seven. Then on Tuesday and Thursday nights, we went to Bible study—in addition to the weeklong revivals we often attended. By the time we drove the forty-five minutes back to our house from all of these services, I was usually fast asleep.

The week we arrived at Pillar of Truth, Bishop Scurry introduced me to her adopted daughter, Penny—newcomers were usually assigned to a member in the church. Penny was a light-skinned tall girl who looked like the bishop, so it wasn't until later that I realized she was adopted; I remember saying to myself, "Wow, her mama is old!" Though Penny was four years older than me, we clicked right away. So one Thursday night after we'd been at the church for a few months, I let her in on some exciting news. "My dad is buying me some clogs," I whispered to her in the pew we shared. "He's getting them in navy—my father loves me in blue." For the following three weeks whenever I'd see Penny, she'd ask, "So did you get the shoes yet?" I shook my head from side to side. On the Sunday morning when I finally showed up in the shoes, Penny was sitting in the pew behind me. "Let me see!" she begged. I beamed as I scooted my right foot back toward her. Penny's eyes widened. "Ooooh, you're going to hell!" she said. Her words stunned me. What was she talking about?

Penny later explained why I was in trouble: "You can't show your feet." The clog covered most of my foot—except for the bottom part of my heel beneath the back strap. After service, when my parents went up to shake Bishop Scurry's hand, I went with them. "Is it okay for me to wear these?" I asked, glancing down toward my shoes. She eyed my clogs for a moment, then looked over at my parents. "She can wear them to school until they're worn out," the bishop said. "But she can't wear them into the house of God." Each time I slid on my clogs in the following weeks, the initial joy I'd felt was eclipsed by fear; apparently, the God of the universe would send me to eternal damnation in a blazing inferno for something as minor as an exposed heel. That's how I began connecting religion, God, and church with judgment, anxiety, and guilt.

EVEN IN SUCH a restrictive church, there was one part of the service I always looked forward to—the music. Every time the choir sang, the harmonious gospel tunes lifted high toward the ceiling and then gently settled, like mist, over the congregation. "Mommy, can I join the choir?" I asked her when I was around seven. "You have to ask the bishop," she told me. On the following Sunday when I made my request, the bishop grinned and kept repeating, "The Sunshine Band"—which was the children's choir. In spite of how strict she was, she was also quite warm and engaging. Every time her lips spread into a grin, I was astonished at how white her teeth were—and this was long before Crest whitening strips.

I was way too young to be in the adult choir—one that sang

"What a Friend We Have in Jesus" so beautifully. I joined the children's choir instead. After just a few weeks of rehearsing with the other kids between Sunday school and morning worship (and by the way, we got two vanilla wafers to tide us over until lunch!), I began to love the Sunshine Band—especially once I was given my first shot at a solo.

If you think my voice is low now, it may surprise you to know that it was even *lower* when I was a kid. "You sound like a man!" my brother, Mikey, would tease me. So on the Sunday when I took the microphone to sing one verse of "Jesus Wants Me for a Sunbeam," the whole church discovered what Mikey already knew: I was the female version of Barry White. "A sunbeam, a sunbeam, Jesus wants me for a sunbeam," I sang, tilting my chin upward, as if that would somehow help me hit the high notes. "A sunbeam, a sunbeam, I'll be a sunbeam for Him." If my solo debut was *terrible,* you wouldn't have known that by the congregation's response: The crowd showered me and the rest of the choir with a round of *Amen!*s and applause. The truth is that no matter how a singer sounded, the members of the congregation were always very encouraging: "Yes, Lawd, that child can sang!"

During my year in the Sunshine Band, I slowly grew comfortable around the other kids—and yet I still never really fit in. We may have all shared the same religion and the same pews every Sunday, but my parents were far more strict than the other parents in the church. In part, that's because they became engulfed in their study of the Old Testament. "The devil is always lurking," Mommy would often say. My mother was more vocal about her beliefs than my father was, but Dad was also 120 percent into it—he eventually became an associate elder at Pillar. Our family would go out into parks and testify, trying to convince people to come to Christ; we were constantly quoting scriptures. Our lives were stripped of anything that could somehow lead us away from God or tempt us to do wrong. Let me explain.

Secular music was considered too "worldly"—we couldn't even sing along to the opening theme song from *The Jeffersons*. Going to see a movie in the theater was a sin (but watching a movie on TV was okay because it had been edited). We also couldn't go roller-skating—the music was evil. Once, my aunt Nita, who saw how music lit me up, offered to play an Al Green record for me on her new hi-fi stereo. Before I could nod my head yes, Mommy gave me a look that said, "Don't even think about it." One thing we were allowed to do was go to amusement parks, like Kings Dominion in Virginia—and these trips were usually fund-raisers for the church. Because there were so few other opportunities for fun, I always looked forward to that.

When it came to all these rules, there were plenty of contradictions: We were allowed to eat grapes, but some of the old-school apostolic church bishops didn't allow their members to do so because the grapes could ferment and become wine; in our religion, drinking any wine or alcohol was considered ungodly—but how could that be true if Jesus once turned water into wine? None of this made sense to me when I was a child. It still doesn't.

The list of restrictions left me and everyone else in the church with basically nothing to do—almost everything fun was off-limits. That might be one reason my parents had so many children—in addition to the fact that women were actually discouraged from using birth control; only the rhythm method was permitted. "God determines birth," Bishop Scurry would remind the adults once the kids had been sent off to the multipurpose room. "Man has nothing to do with it." Though my parents clearly lived by this principle, there were times when my father seemed a little embarrassed to have so many children. When anyone would mention how large our family was, I noticed that he often averted his eyes.

But my parents wanted all of us to go to heaven—and following a set of legalistic rules was how they believed they could make that happen. If we lived a structured life on earth, we would live a better one in eternity. They taught us that the rapture could come at any moment, and if we weren't living right, we would all go straight to hell. The goal was to be "saved" and to stay that way by staying obedient. And being saved involved being baptized and speaking in tongues—you had to do both. Our bishop often quoted Acts 2:38: "Then Peter said unto them, Repent, and be baptized every one of you in the name of Jesus Christ for the remission of sins, and ye shall receive the gift of the Holy Ghost." Another passage we often frequently heard was Acts 2:4: "And they were all filled with the Holy Ghost, and began to speak with other tongues, as the Spirit gave them utterance." Speaking in tongues was considered evidence that you were truly a Christian and on your way to heaven—because you were already speaking the heavenly tongue. That guaranteed your seat in the kingdom.

I will always remember the Sunday I tried to get saved. A few months before, I'd already been baptized. That meant that I was ready for stage two of salvation—speaking in tongues. For months, I'd been admiring a woman in our congregation who spoke in tongues so eloquently. I imagined what it would feel like to have such beautiful foreign words fall from my lips. So during the seven P.M. service, I dropped down to my knees and I tarried—which I thought meant praying until white matter from my spit formed around the edges of my mouth . . . that's what I'd seen the adults do. With my eyes closed real tight, I begged God to give me the gift of the spirit. I stayed down there at the side of the pew until I developed a little headache, but nothing happened—and I do mean *nothing*. So I faked it—I was eight and a half years old. I let out a string of sentences—a few Spanish-sounding words mixed with some dippity-doo-dah nonsense—and I pretended it was all inspired by the Holy Ghost. In my heart, I knew it was wrong. But I wanted so badly to fit in, to be like the others in our church who were saved. Afterward, I stood up and testified. "I thank the Lord for being here," I recited from memory, "and I thank Him for my health and strength. All those who know the words of prayer, please pray my strength in the Lord. Today, I received the gift of the Holy Spirit. I am saved." Some people clapped, others cried. And I lived in fear that if the rapture came suddenly, God would know I had pretended and would condemn me to hell—a place filled with brimstone that was hotter than fire. For years, I carried around that feeling: I'd often think, *I need to really get saved before the rapture, because God knows that I faked it.*

We finally left Pillar of Truth when I was ten. Mommy and Bishop Scurry got into a disagreement about something the bishop claimed.

"Even Jesus was imperfect," said Bishop Scurry. "Jesus was both spirit and man, wrapped in flesh. When he was young, He probably got in trouble for stealing cookies from the cookie jar."

"That's not true," Mommy said insistently. "Jesus was perfect." That difference of opinion escalated into a full-blown conflict. Whatever led to our departure a few Sundays later, I don't think Bishop Scurry was sad to see us go—I got the feeling she didn't like my mother very much.

We may have moved to a different church, but we didn't stray from our extremely religious lifestyle. My parents began attending the church of a minister who'd already left Pillar to start her own congregation in the basement of some building. Our new pastor, Bishop Bellamy, was just as strict as the former one—and we were only there for about a year before another argument erupted. My parents owned a living room set that the bishop disapproved of. "The colors are red and black," she told them, "and that makes it like the devil. You have to get rid of it." The bishop told her exactly which Dumpster she should dump it in. That's why Mommy believed that the pastor simply wanted her new couch and love seat—and rather than giving it up, she and my father left the congregation.

Once I was grown, I finally asked my parents why they first joined Pillar of Truth. "When they greeted us for the first time, they just showed us so much love," Mommy said. "They always made us feel like part of their family." But what is true in many families was also true at Pillar: The ties that bound us together became the ties that strangled us.

As traumatic as that whole experience was for me, I believe that my parents were doing what they thought was best for our family. In the seventies—a decade when so many Americans got caught up in various religious doctrines—my parents became convinced that staying loyal to a set of bylaws would keep all of us on the path to God. Yet in the years after we left both of those congregations, even my parents would come to realize what my aunts already knew—our family had fallen into religious extremism.

CHAPTER 4

"Homey Toni Braxton"

I call it the "covered wagon syndrome": What happened in the Braxton house stayed in the Braxton house. My parents, who have always been very private, didn't want their children talking publicly about our family issues; the years we spent inside that church reinforced that tendency. That's one of the reasons I never felt like I could relate to other children—especially at school.

During my elementary school years, my teachers would organize a Halloween march; all the kids would excitedly put on their costumes and parade around the halls. "Where's your costume?" one of my classmates asked me when I was in fifth grade. "Oh, I didn't bring one," I said. The truth was that my family didn't acknowledge any holiday, even after we left Pillar of Truth—but since I already felt like an oddball, I certainly didn't want to admit that. Thankfully, my teacher always brought extra costumes for any child who had forgotten one, so I pretended this was the case for me and put on the princess tiara and skirt she handed me. Once I was home, I didn't dare reveal to Mommy that I'd worn the costume because I knew I'd be in trouble.

My classmates teased me mercilessly. "Hey, homey Toni Braxton!" they'd yell out in the hallways and on the playground. Not only did I wear a dress every single day of the year (yes, even when it was snowing . . .), but my outfits were unstylish (as in homely and frumpy . . . or, as my classmates put it, "homey"); what's worse, Mommy usually swept my fine, pressed, and curled hair into a little ponytail that sat squarely on top of my head. And it didn't help that my family had so many children—the year I was ten, my sister Tamar, the youngest, had already arrived. That made us look like the weirdo religious family who apparently didn't practice birth control. In the tree-hugging seventies, you can imagine how many stares we got.

My homework was often neglected. We spent so many hours in church that there just wasn't enough time to complete all of my assignments. "Why aren't you getting your work done?" my parents would ask, making a fuss. I'd shrug and take the licking that came next. On the one hand, my parents didn't play when it came to requiring my siblings and me to do well academically; but on the other hand, they didn't make our schoolwork a priority. The priority was memorizing scriptures and attending services to focus on my studies. At church, all of us children were given batches of twenty-six scriptures to memorize, organized from A to Z; every Thursday night in our testimony service, we each had to stand up and quote that week's designated verse. "The Lord is my Shepherd, I shall not want," I'd recite from Psalm 23. "He maketh me to lie down in green pastures; He leadeth me beside the still waters; He restoreth my soul." By the time I was twelve, I could recite literally dozens of scriptures perfectly from my memory. Yet I was a C student.

One day when my class was scheduled to take the Maryland School Assessment, the state's standardized test, my teacher noticed that I wasn't eating lunch at school. "Why aren't you eating?" she asked. "Because we're fasting at church," I told her. A couple of times a year and especially during Lent and Passover, we refrained from eating for a week or two (though Mommy would always break down and give us dinner). We were told that fasting was a way to draw closer to God. When I explained this to my teacher, her eyes widened, and I could see the creases form on her forehead. "Well, you need to eat in order to be ready for your test," she said. She then reached into her bag and gave me a vanilla bar. "Thank you," I murmured. With every bite I took of the bar, I felt more and more guilty. I never told my parents that I ate the bar, because I knew they'd be upset.

My favorite subject was reading. I loved a series titled *The Boxcar Children* by Gertrude Chandler Warner. I must've read every book in the set dozens of times. In it, the writer tells the story of four orphaned children who create a home for themselves in an abandoned boxcar in the forest; their grandfather eventually discovers them there and rescues them. Every summer, the children then go on all kinds of adventures together and solve mysteries. My parents usually only read the Bible to us when I was small, so I read the books on my own. I'd curl up on a fluffy pillow on my bed, turn the pages one by one, and imagine that I was the fifth boxcar child.

Other than excelling in reading, social studies, and chorus (which was effortless for me!), I was an average student. When I was in fourth grade, my homeroom teacher once sat me in the back of the class, in a corner by myself, because I hadn't completed my homework for the third time that month. I sat quietly and stared out the window as she taught at the chalkboard. Later, all the other kids pulled out a packet she'd apparently given them earlier, when I was out sick with asthma (yes, I had that, too). I didn't have a packet to review—but since I was already in trouble, I was scared to raise my hand and ask for a copy. Over the next two weeks, the teacher continued reviewing the packet that I was missing, and I just fiddled with my other papers and pretended that I was following along. Of course, I didn't tell my parents about it, though I knew that falling behind would get me in more trouble. But if I'd gone home and mentioned the missing packet, my parents would've been like, "Why didn't you get the packet in the first place? You must've done something wrong." It was easier to stay silent.

My best subject was math—I consistently earned B-pluses.

So like some of the other students in my fifth-grade class, I wanted to begin algebra early, which would've been in the fall of sixth grade. "Can I try algebra next year?" I asked my teacher. "No, Toni," she said, hardly even glancing up from the papers she was grading at her desk. "You need an A to start algebra early." In that instance, I should've marched right home and told Mommy what happened—she probably would've gone up to that school and acted a fool in order to get me into that math class. But I could never gauge when my mother would be upset with me. I was so conditioned to believe that everything I did was somehow a sin. I was always hearing that God was a God of wrath—and that meant He was judging everything I did.

I've always known that both my parents would do anything to protect me. Yet my childhood was filled with so many gray areas: Should I bring someone else's behavior to my parents' attention so that they could step in, or would I be accused of doing something wrong? Most of the time, I feared that if I spoke up, a situation would be declared my fault. I walked around with this feeling in my gut that I was about to be punished for *something*. In church, I often prayed that God would forgive me for a list of "sins" I probably never even committed. And of course I couldn't tell anyone outside of my family what I was experiencing. In the covered wagon, the Braxtons lived by a single commandment: Shut your mouth and suppress whatever you feel. I didn't know it then, but that was the perfect preparation for the life that awaited me.

. . .

ONCE WE FLED those two repressive churches, we joined Truth Foundation on Charles Street in Baltimore. I was about twelve then. We'd attended that church sporadically up until I was about six and a half, and my parents had remained friendly with the head minister, Pastor Doughty. Though the church was also Apostolic, the pastor wasn't nearly as strict as Bishop Scurry had been. So when we returned there, I could exhale—but only halfway, because we brought some of our habits with us. My parents had been so influenced by Pillar that they still wouldn't allow us to listen to secular music, celebrate holidays, or wear pants.

By the time we became part of Truth Foundation, Mommy had realized her children could harmonize. You might've heard the story about the day that Tamar—who noticed that we'd run out of toilet paper—sang out from the bathroom, "Somebody bring me some toilet paper!" I wasn't actually there that day, but one by one, my other sisters gathered and turned Tamar's refrain into a perfect harmony. My mother overheard this and decided she should organize us into an official group. So at home, Mommy, who served as the choir director at every church we attended, began lining us up near her piano and making us practice for hours. Then on Sundays, we'd perform songs like "If You're Happy and You Know It," as well as hymns. Mommy made sure our harmonies were flawless.

My mother is Joe Jackson's first cousin. I'm joking, of

course, but only a little—because Mommy sure was serious about our harmonizing. If we sang a chord wrong, for instance, she would let us know—and for some reason, Towanda got it the worst. To avoid Mommy's disapproving eye, I practiced a lot on my own . . . And did I mention that my mom's maiden name is Jackson?

When I was ten, we moved from our town house to a ranch rambler. In that house, I began taking piano lessons—we had a French provincial upright piano trimmed in gold. Mommy was breeding me as the piano player for the Braxton family. My piano teacher was David, a man from our church who recognized my potential as a musician and simply wanted to help me. My parents would give him three or four dollars when he stopped by for our lesson each week. Sometimes, he didn't ask for a dime—or else he'd say to my dad, "Can I just get a few dollars for gas?" He was the nicest man.

At first, I didn't want to learn to play the way classically trained musicians do, which is by practicing scales; instead, I wanted to jump ahead and play the chords that I heard pianists in church playing. But I did continue my lessons for about four years, and along the way, I started picking things up naturally. When my sisters and I performed around town, I always served as our accompanist. I didn't play all that well at first—that's why we often sang a lot of a cappella harmonies, in a similar style to those of the gospel group Take 6. And since I couldn't yet play and sing a solo at the same time (that takes years of practice!), I was really just one voice in the mix of five. The first song I later learned to play and sing simultaneously was "Goin' Up Yonder." From there, I got good at gospel songs like "God Is" and "I Am Grateful."

During those years, I fell in love with music. Because so much of it was forbidden in our household, I'd sneak and listen to secular songs on the radio. I could tell you anything you wanted to know about a song—the bass line, the drum line, the harmonies on the top and the bottom. And I loved all kinds of music: I relished the Fleetwood Mac tunes our bus driver played as he drove us to school. I even practiced singing when I was by myself. I'd grab a ketchup bottle from our pantry and practice in the mirror. "Shame!" I sang, trying to mimic Evelyn "Champagne" King's voice. "Burning, you keep my whole body yearning! You got me so confused, it's a shame!" I'd shake and swivel my body across the bedroom in the same way that she did onstage. I wanted to be exactly like her.

The first time I heard Anita Baker sing, I just about fainted. One morning while I was standing at the bus stop, my neighbor across the street began playing a record from the soul/funk band Chapter 8, which featured Anita as a lead vocalist. "Can I borrow that record?" I later asked my neighbor. I then smuggled it into my house, waited till Mommy was at the store, and played the entire vinyl on our record player. "I just want to be your girl," she crooned in her smoky, molasses-tinged, androgynous tone that sounded as if it had been in a compressor. It was the first time I'd heard a soloist whose voice had the same texture and timbre as mine. I didn't ever want to return the vinyl to my neighbor.

Grease was also big for me. When that musical hit theaters in 1978, I couldn't go to the movies to see it because our religion considered that a sin—surprise, surprise. But I still caught a few pieces of certain songs because everybody around me was singing them. In front of my bedroom mirror, I practiced the big hit by John Travolta and Olivia Newton-John: "You're the one that I want—ooh, ooh, ooh!"

The songs of the seventies infused the entire country with a certain vitality and joy—yet for me, music did far more than that. Hearing it made me sure that I wanted to be part of creating it. I could literally lose myself in the chords; a great song had the power to transport me to another place—to make me remember the best of who I was and to forget the things that brought me pain. All at once, I felt this amazing sense of profound fulfillment, as if an unscratchable itch had suddenly been relieved. Whenever I sang the first note of a song, I was hopeful. I was no longer that square religious girl who wore skirts down past her knees. I instead became the person I yearned to be. The cool girl. The popular kid. The beautiful one. The star.

OUR FAMILY GATHERED for dinner every night at six. Mommy began preparing the meal around the time I got home from school at three P.M.—and I was always her little helper.

"Set the table," she'd tell me. I'd carefully pull down our stack of plates (olive green trimmed in blue . . . hey, it was the seventies!) and place each one around our table. The aroma of savory meatloaf with gravy, garlic potatoes, sautéed cabbage, and homemade butter biscuits rose from the oven and wafted throughout the house. Two Maxwell House cans sat atop Mommy's gas stove—one for pork grease, one for chicken. She'd use the leftover oil to flavor everything from pork chops and vegetables to smothered chicken. It may not have been totally healthy, but it was the best Southern cooking you could find. "Is your mama making cheese biscuits tonight?" a neighbor would often ask me. In Severn, my mother's recipes were legendary.

As Mommy finished dinner, I helped my younger sisters with their homework. I was around ten when my older cousin Kimmy left our home and returned to live with her family— and that's when I really began to feel like the eldest. I became the second mom: I helped my mother chop and dice vegetables, I washed dishes (I was the official dishwasher—and let me tell you, we had a ton of dishes!), and I vacuumed the house. I also oversaw my younger siblings. "Did you finish your math assignment?" I'd ask Traci or Towanda. Because I was so much older than the other girls—I am five years older than the next sister, Traci, and a decade older than the youngest, Tamar—I felt more like their parent than their sibling. Mikey and I are only two years apart, but since he's a boy, he got out of some of the domestic chores. That was considered women's work. He did at least have to take out the trash.

Just before six, my father arrived home from E.J. Korvettes. We all lived on my father's one income—which means my parents were very clever about how they used their money. Every Sunday when the newspaper arrived, my siblings and I would sit at our table and clip out all the coupons. We were far from wealthy (Dad once told me it would take him six years to earn $100,000), and yet we always seemed to have everything we needed, mostly thanks to how well my parents economized. My mother managed the weekly budget and used about $100 a week for groceries. Mom would go to this store called Maurry's Steak House and buy what seemed like a quarter of a cow and store it in our upright freezer. She bought a lot of food on sale and froze it—which is how we saved a lot of money.

My parents also had very good credit—so they were able to get a loan for the town house. As for the extras we always seemed to have, Dad's job came with plenty of perks: The employees at E.J. Korvettes got household items like televisions and microwaves at a steep discount. It didn't hurt that my parents had inherited a piece of land and a house when they were married. That left them with enough money to care for our family, give to the church (my parents tithed 10 percent of their income), and even save up for a few luxuries (like our piano). By the way they managed their money, my parents passed on one lesson to me early: As important as it is to save, you should also spend and enjoy a portion of what you have. For instance, even when things were tight in our house, my parents would still set aside enough money for our family to go to an amusement park or on a road trip. And every week after Mom had written out the checks for all of our bills, she'd always leave herself with a few dollars for something she wanted for herself—like a new pair of panty hose.

Though my father was officially the head of the house-hold, we all knew that Mommy was really in charge, especially regarding anything related to the house or us children. She simply had the loudest voice and the strongest opinions. Yet once Daddy got home and we all took our places around the table, he did sit at the head of the table, say grace over the food, and lead the dinnertime conversation. "We put up a new display at the store today," he'd tell us. After giving us the full update on his day and listening to Mom's, he'd sometimes turn to me and ask, "So what happened at school today?" I'd mutter a couple of sentences before stuffing the edge of a biscuit into my mouth.

Once I cleared the table and helped Mommy put away the food, my parents would often call us into the living room. "We need to pray right now," Mommy would say. We prayed about everything—from an issue happening in the church to some struggle that had arisen in my parents' lives. Sometime during the evening, Mommy would use her favorite line at least once: "The devil is raging." I think my parents really feared that Satan was right there in the room, trying to overtake us. During our days at Pillar of Truth, Bishop Scurry would often oversee exorcisms, during which we'd cast demons out of people. Afterward, we'd all gather, hold hands, and pray that the spirits that left those people's bodies didn't get into ours. In 1977, my parents might have physically moved on from Pillar, but spiritually and emotionally, they were still quite connected to what we learned there.

Before bedtime, Mommy would occasionally pull out her gospel vinyl records and play either a Mahalia Jackson or James Cleveland eight-track. "Jesus is the best thing that ever happened to me," sang Reverend Cleveland in that thick, husky voice that sounded as if it came from another world; his accompanying choir called out their agreement with a flurry of *amen*s. "Jesus is the best thing that ever happened to me." I loved that style of music so much because it seemed closer to secular—and that made me feel closer to normal. What I didn't know is that it was a remake of Gladys Knight's song "You're the Best Thing That Ever Happened to Me." With every soulful note that lifted from Mommy's record player, I was smitten. The piano. The drums. The tambourines. The spirit. It all filled a space inside of me that only music could. Even way back then, I somehow sensed that. I'm still certain of it today.

CHAPTER 5

Levi's and Puppy Love

Designer jeans were all the rage in the early eighties—Jordache, Sasson, Calvin Klein. So you can imagine how excited I was when my cousin Felicia gave me a pair of original 501 button-fly Levi's. I was fourteen—and my eighth-grade classmates had never seen me in pants, much less fashionable ones. On the day I got the secondhand jeans, I closed my bedroom door, slipped one leg at a time into the jeans, and quickly fastened each button. The Levi's were a little big on me, which made them a perfect fit. Before Mommy could open the door and catch me wearing pants, I pulled them off and buried them in my bottom drawer. Every day for a week, I took them out and tried them on, just so I could practice what it would feel like to wear pants.

One evening in December 1980, a huge snowstorm hit Severn. As the temperature dipped into the teens, my big opportunity arose. "Mommy," I whispered just before bedtime, "do you think I could wear pants tomorrow? It's supposed to be very cold."

"You got pants?" Mommy snapped.

"Yes, because Felicia gave me a pair," I admitted. "I have them in my drawer."

Mommy studied my face for several seconds. "No you can't," she said. "You know we don't wear pants around here. Put on two pair of tights if you're that cold."

The following day, the snow continued falling. I don't know where my courage came from, but I again asked my mother if I could wear the jeans. She ignored me. Then on the third day of the storm—on a morning when the wind chill factor was in the single digits—I repeated my request. My mother, who was combing Towanda's hair for school, was in my room.

"Mommy, can I wear the pants today?"

She glared at me. "You want to wear the darn pants?" she finally shouted. "Then wear the darn pants!" She then stormed out of my bedroom and into hers—and I thought she was going to call my father.

Before Mommy could change her mind, I went over to the dresser and pulled out the Levi's. As I put them on, I repeated to myself, "I'm not going to feel guilty." Because of what I'd been taught, I truly believed I'd go to hell if I wore the jeans. But that fear wasn't strong enough to eclipse my exhilaration.

Once I buttoned the Levi's, I then put on a plaid button-up top and brown leather boots with tassels on the front. I arranged my hair into a snatch-back, a layered style with two pink combs at the sides of my head. I then glided over to my bedroom mirror and peered at my reflection. For the first time in my life, I felt fashionable.

When Mommy spotted me on the way out the front door, she didn't say a word—but her chilly gaze told me she disapproved. I rushed out and made my way to the bus stop. I saw a few of my classmates huddled together, trying to keep warm. "Who's that?" someone said as I approached. Once I got close enough for them to see my face, one of them yelled out, "Oh my God—Toni Braxton got on pants!" All I could do was stand there and beam. Once I boarded the bus, everyone stopped, stared, and drew in a collective gasp. "Wow," said a kid in the front row, "she's wearing pants!" In that moment and for the rest of the school day, I felt famous. And above all else, I felt like I fit in.

The next morning, I put on the same jeans. In fact, I wore them every day until it was summer. At school, a girl named Cheryl came up to me in the hall. "I ain't sayin' no names," she said, "but someone told me you wear the same pants every day."

I smirked. "I have several pair of the pants," I lied. She gave me a look that said, "Yeah, right."

After I'd worn the pants for a whole week, Mommy intervened: "I said you could wear those pants for one day because it was cold." That's how my modeling spree ended.

In a sense, that episode marked a beginning. Six weeks later, my mother actually bought me a pantsuit. "You can only wear it when it's cold outside," she told me. Later that same year, she also bought me a tube of lip gloss and pale pink nail polish. "This is only for special occasions," she said. I wasn't sure what "special occasions" she had in mind, but I wasn't going to argue it. Little by little, my mother was changing. For me—the awkward religious girl who'd never felt cute—that shift couldn't happen fast enough.

I LOVED TELEVISION. By the time I was in junior high, our family owned four TV sets that Dad had brought home from Korvettes. We had one in the family room downstairs (a color console!), one in my brother's room, and another in my parents' room; the fourth was in the kitchen. I eventually moved the kitchen TV into my bedroom, which is where it stayed. By then, my parents still weren't allowing us to listen to secular music, but they did let us watch television. They knew that by the time a movie appeared on TV several years after it had been released in the theaters, the cursing and other offensive material had usually been edited out. Yet once I had a TV in my room, I managed to sneak in some programs that my parents considered too worldly.

Like *Solid Gold*—a TV series that debuted in 1980. Every Saturday, I sat in awe of the show's dancers, who pranced around in flashy costumes as the week's top hits played. The first season was hosted by Dionne Warwick, and in the premiere episode, Irene Cara belted out her hit "Fame." I was hooked from the first note. I also loved *American Bandstand*. The DeBarges, a family singing group, once performed on that show. The whole time I watched, I thought, *Maybe the family-singing-group thing is okay*. Maybe I could be cool after all.

My all-time favorite show was *Soul Train*. Every week, I saw black artists who looked like me—and watching them perform on TV was very different from just hearing them on the radio. All the big stars were on there: the Jacksons, Luther Vandross, Rick James, Johnny Gill, Stacy Lattisaw. Janet Jackson once came on the show to sing "Don't Stand Another Chance." With every tilt of her head, her hair bounced like Tootie's on *The Facts of Life*. I paid attention to those kinds of details, especially when it came to the young singers. And I never missed an episode. Every Saturday, my parents took a forty-five-minute drive to Baltimore so they could go to the farmers' market—and I knew that gave me two to three hours to watch *Soul Train* in peace.

By the early eighties, stars like Donna Summer and Diana Ross were on all of the music shows I watched. I wanted large eyeballs like Diana's. I also imagined what I'd look like in the gaucho pants that Donna often strutted around in onstage. The big hair, the double-knit jersey fabrics, the cute sandals with the toes out—I longed for the glamour of the big stars. I also dreamed of becoming a famous soloist, but that didn't seem possible because I was always singing with my family. In the African-American community, a certain idea has persisted for generations: If one gets, we all get. We're all in the boat together, so we must all get out together. In my family, it was taboo to separate from the group. But secretly, that's exactly what I wanted to do. I didn't simply want to be an extension of my parents and siblings. I wanted to be an individual. I wanted to be like Donna and Diana.

AS I TRIED to leave my "Homey Toni Braxton" days behind, I studied fashion. One of my aunts kept a stack of *Ebony* magazines in her living room, and I often leafed through the issues. In those days, *Ebony* was known for an event called Fashion Fair—a traveling runway show that featured black models wearing vibrant outfits, flawless makeup, and chocolate-colored lipstick; when the magazine's editors included coverage of Fashion Fair in their pages, I cut out my favorite looks. All the teasing I got from my classmates had left me with something to prove—that I could be stylish. I'm not really a vengeful person, but in the back of my head, I was always thinking, *I'll show them.*

And yet the change in my image happened *veeeeery* slowly—which means the cruelty from my classmates continued. "I ain't sayin' no names," one girl would spout off to another in the hallway, "but somebody was talkin' 'bout you."

"You'd better tell me who it was," the other kid would shout, "or I'm gonna beat you up!"

Somehow, the finger of blame would always end up pointed directly at me; the irony was that I wasn't talking to anyone about anything, because I'd always been in the out crowd. Even still, girls would randomly come up to me and hit me in the head or push me down and say, "I heard you was talkin' 'bout me!" I might've been under five feet and scrawny, but I wasn't a punk. "I don't know you well enough to talk about you!" I shot back. They probably knew that—but they picked on me because my presence irritated them. Once when I came home and told Mommy how the other kids were treating me, she said, "Nobody is greater than you but God. They're just jealous." I really believed that. I might've been the odd girl out, but I still had an air about me, and the kids at school could sense that.

Later, when some of my other classmates went up to a girl named Tammy—a school bully—they told her that I'd been talking smack about her. She goes, "Toni Braxton? She doesn't talk to anybody! Ya'll lying on that girl!" From that point on, my classmates began giving me a little less of a hard time.

My best friend was Kim White. Actually, our friendship began on a sour note: Back in fifth grade, Kim was teasing me at school one day because of the way I was dressed. "You're so country!" she shouted, snickering. Kim was one of the cutest and most popular girls in school, and that made her teasing even more painful. "Where did you get that dress from— your mama's closet?" That evening, I went home and told my mother what happened. "Kim White said that to you? I know her mother," Mommy said. Kim's mom was in my mother's wedding. "Let me call her and handle this." The intervention apparently worked. The next day, Kim was suddenly nice, and we've been friends ever since. We came from similar backgrounds: all her siblings' names started with the letter K, like the Kardashians: Kim, Kelly, Kristy, and Kia. And like me, she was the eldest in her family, so we bonded over that. When it came to fashion, however, Kim and I were worlds apart: She dressed her butt off. She also had great hair and a very cute face. Boys always liked her—and even if a guy did look at me, everyone was like, "Wow—I can't believe he likes Toni over Kim." At first the comparisons bothered me, but I learned to ignore them. Plus, I was just happy to be hanging out with a popular girl. Of course, that didn't exactly make me popular—but it did mean that I was seen as little more acceptable (and slightly less teasable!) in the eyes of my other classmates.

I didn't have a boyfriend at that point—I was in junior high before I started really noticing boys. This girl named Tammy had a cousin that I thought was *sooooo* cute—and I confessed my crush to her. "He kind of likes you, too," Tammy told me. The following spring when we were all at a pool party (my parents only let me go because they knew the other kids' parents were church folk . . .), the boy and I started flirting around. At the end of the evening, we kissed—and a few seconds after our lips met, he stuck his tongue in my mouth! *What the heck was that?* I thought. I'd seen my mom and dad kiss, of course, but there was never any tongue involved. "You can't kiss," he said to me afterward. I was mortified. Later, when I told Tammy what happened, she said, "You have to learn how to kiss." She pulled a doll from my little sister's bed and said, "Here, let's practice on this." Tammy then slowly stuck her tongue in and out of the doll's mouth. *Ick*. I didn't even want to try that.

Among my classmates, I was usually the last one to do anything, so of course, I was also the last one to get my period. As I awaited its arrival, I started reading *Are You There God? It's Me, Margaret*. I absolutely loved Judy Blume's book, and I read it over and over again. I could relate to everything that twelve-year-old Margaret, the main character, was going through: waiting and waiting for her period to come, wearing her first bra, being part of the itty bitty titty committee, having a crush on boys, and eventually dealing with a maxi pad wedged between her thighs. In a nutshell, that was my life. My mother had talked to me about my period a little ("When you get your menstrual," she'd say, "it makes you a woman"), but for the most part, I learned about it by reading an encyclopedia. The day I finally spotted red in my panties, I went to my mother.

"Mommy, I'm bleeding a little bit," I said.

"Where?" she said.

"Down there," I said, pointing toward my crotch.

She paused. "You haven't been messing around with any little boys, have you?"

"No," I said, shaking my head and wondering what the heck she was talking about.

"Well congratulations," she finally said as she pulled me close for a hug. "You're becoming a woman."

Soon after, Mommy showed me how to use pads. The huge maxi pad was a little awkward, but wearing it made me feel very grown-up. "You have to be responsible with your things," said Mommy, who went on to explain that I'd have to carry a purse to school with my pads in it. And the instructions didn't end there: A couple days later when she saw me take a bite of a tuna fish sandwich, she stopped me. "Uh-uh—you can't eat fish of any kind while you're on your menstrual cycle," she said. "The smell will come through your pores. Don't take baths either—only showers. And don't eat anything cold because it'll make you cramp more." And then there was the most important rule of all: Tampons were 100 percent prohibited.

"What do you got this for?" Mommy asked when she once found a tampon in my room.

"My friend gave it to me," I said.

"That's 'cause that child's doing other things!" Mommy said. By the time I wore my first tampon, I was in college.

To this day, I have no idea where Mommy's rules came from, but here's one thing I can tell you—my mother was doing her best to prepare me for womanhood. Her little "You haven't been messing around with any little boys" comment was probably born of fear—she didn't want her little girl, her firstborn, to grow up too fast or lose her innocence too early. No mother has a handbook on parenting; most of us are just repeating what our mothers passed on to us. Now that I'm a mother myself, I understand that. If only I'd known that at fourteen.

. . .

THE SUMMER BEFORE I entered high school, I got my first job—I worked as a custodian at a school. I only earned minimum wage (a whopping $3.35 an hour!), but I was thrilled to have my own money coming in. When I got my second check, I went out and bought new towels and accessories for our bathroom. I put the rest of the money into a savings account. A few weeks before I started high school, Mommy said I could use some of that savings to buy school clothes. So I went to a fashion store and picked out a pair of white argyle pants—by this time, Mommy had eased up enough for me to risk bringing home pants. I also bought myself a pair of brown leather penny loafers, a huge trend by the early eighties. I really wanted to slide a quarter into my loafers but my shoes were too small for that—size five and a half.

Once I got to high school, I started noticing boys. My first boyfriend was Ferron. He had fair skin and gorgeous green eyes, and though he was bowlegged and not very tall, I thought he was handsome. Plus, he was preapproved: He lived two houses down, and my parents knew his parents. In fact, our families were related through marriage: My uncle Ro Ro and Ferron's grandfather were brothers. That didn't surprise me, because everybody in our neighborhood was related in some kind of way. And since we were neighbors, we'd known each other for years—in fact, he teased me at school until my mother called his mother, and his mom told him,

"Stop teasing that Braxton girl." He did—and by ninth grade, I had a crush on him.

When Ferron eventually asked me to be his girlfriend, I giddily accepted. We kissed and made out while our parents were out of sight, but we both knew it wasn't going much farther than that. While we were fooling around, he'd touch my butt and boobies—not that I had any boobies at the time. "Stop it," I'd say, pushing his hand away. He always did. But over time, he got frustrated that we didn't go farther—so he broke up with me. "I'm a growing boy," he told me. "I have needs." I was devastated. I even turned to Mommy for comfort. "Ferron and I broke up," I told her, my eyes welling with water. "It's all right," Mommy said, embracing me fully. Once I gave her the details, I'm pretty sure my mother wanted to kill him.

During high school, I actually started to feel somewhat normal. In tenth grade, I befriended Angie Buck, an athletic type who was very popular on campus. Angie's cliques became my cliques—and I suddenly got a whole new group of friends by association. But even after Angie introduced me to some of the cool kids, I was still seen as a little geeky—old perceptions die hard.

In eleventh grade, Ferron and I began dating again—but we broke it off again a few months later. By the time the senior prom rolled around, we had a little bit of a rekindle—which is why we decided to go to the senior prom together. Do you want to hear something cheesy? We actually discussed who would pay for the prom. "I'll rent the car," he said, negotiating, "and buy the pictures. We'll split the cost of the tickets." I ended up paying for much more than the pictures, but for some reason, I went along with it.

I designed my own dress. It was a taffeta number that had sequins, a belt, and a big fan on the side—just like the one I'd seen an Ebony Fashion Fair model wear. I saved $75 to buy the fabric. Miss Margaret, a lady in my neighborhood who was like an aunt, sewed the dress for me. I completed my look with a pair of elbow-length white gloves, white stockings, and some $60 heels I bought at the Wild Pair. In 1984, everybody wanted to look like Madonna—and in that dress, I felt like the black version of her. You couldn't tell me I didn't look good!

Ferron pulled up to my house in a Cadillac that he borrowed from his father—so much for paying to rent a car. Once inside, he greeted my parents, and then he turned to me and said, "You look nice." The night went downhill from there. At the prom, we only danced with each other for a few songs before Ferron went off to dance with another girl—and not just any girl, but Sharron, the girl he'd dated on and off since junior high. I told Angie what was happening, and much to my alarm, she said something to the girl. "I'm not trying to take Ferron away from you," the girl later told me. "We just danced when our song came on." Her explanation only made me feel worse—and I was very upset at Angie for telling her what I'd said.

My curfew was midnight—my father had made that clear.

So when I realized that I might not make it home in time (the prom was kinda far out in Baltimore), I called my dad at eleven P.M. After the usual third degree ("Where are you? Who are you with? What's happening?"), Daddy finally agreed that I could get home a little late. All my other friends were planning to hang out for the rest of the night and then drive to Kings Dominion amusement park the following morning. Ferron was also going. Even my friend Kim was going—and my parents would sometimes allow me to do things if Kim was involved. But not this time: During my last year of high school, Mommy and Daddy were in a "no" phase. I think they were afraid that I might have sex—and they regarded my vagina as theirs. Ferron dropped me off at my front door at 12:17 A.M.

A couple days later when I saw Ferron at school, he came up to me. "I'm so sorry," he said. "I didn't mean to hurt you." But that didn't change the reality: My first love had become my first heartbreak. And on top of it all, I had to shell out my hard-earned cash for our hideous pictures and even for the tickets—Ferron was supposed to give me his half for our tickets, but he never did. Unbelievable.

DURING MY SENIOR year, my father became the pastor of Mount Tabor, a United Methodist church in Crownsville, Maryland. In the months leading up to his appointment, Dad had already been preaching sermons all over town; my sisters and I were his opening act. By then, my brother, Mikey, had found a way to get out of singing with the family. Once he was in high school, he signed up for a vocational medical program, and that meant he had to work on the weekends. Lucky him.

The inside of our new church looked exactly like the one in *The Color Purple*. The sanctuary was small, with two sets of pews lined up on either side of a prominent middle aisle. There was even a little balcony. A couple summers before when my father had visited this church to preach, I remember saying to myself, "This is so cute—I wish my dad could pastor a church like this." So I was excited when he actually became the minister there. Up in the pulpit, my father looked so respectable in his clergyman's collar.

Daddy was a great preacher. There wasn't a whole lot of shouting or jumping around during his sermons—that wasn't his style. He was more of a straightforward teacher, a Joel Osteen type whose messages were very informative and inspiring. My mother sometimes spoke in the church, too: She was an evangelist. The Sunday service often ended the way it began—my sisters and I stood to deliver a pitch-perfect version of an old hymn like "Blessed Assurance" or "What a Friend We Have in Jesus."

My experience in Dad's church was nothing like it had been at Pillar of Truth: I regularly wore pants and lip gloss to school, and long gone were the days when the congregation would gather to cast out demons. And yet even as my parents gradually became more lenient, in some ways, they were still very stern. One night, I fell asleep listening to Rick James—I had hidden the cassette recorder under my pillow. The next morning when my mother noticed the music, she confronted me. "If you keep listening to that devil music, that rock and roll, you'll mess around and you could die in your sleep next time. You don't want to go to hell listening to that music." That scared me. Even now, I don't listen to music before bedtime.

As I share this and so many of the other episodes from my childhood, my intention isn't to shame either one of my parents—it is to finally free myself by standing in my own truth. Healing begins with acknowledgment. I absolutely know that Mommy and Daddy love me. They always have and always will. But here's what I also know: The people who love us the most can also unintentionally wound us.

CHAPTER 6

Miracle at Amoco

Singing has always been my Plan A. By the time I graduated from Glen Burnie High School in 1984, my sisters and I were seasoned singers who'd performed at just about every church in our area. I had a solo part here and there, but mostly, I continued to sing with the group and play the piano. Yet more and more, I longed to become a famous soloist. And if that dream didn't pan out, I had a Plan B: After college, I'd marry a doctor or a senator and become a strong wife. That sounds a little crazy to me now, but at seventeen, it somehow made perfect sense.

After high school, I stayed with my family and enrolled in community college. As a high school graduation gift, Dad bought me a blue Honda Civic CRX with gold and silver highlights on the sides. I had "TOO CUTE" put onto the license plate because I thought the car was just adorable. I was ecstatic to get my own wheels—if I couldn't live on my own, at least I could drive myself around.

During my last year of high school, I'd started dating a guy who was a few years older than me—in a moment, you'll understand why I'll simply call him Trevor, which is not his real name. Given the childhood I lived through, I'm sure you can see why just the mention of sex filled me with guilt. It felt like a dirty word. In our house, nice Christian girls kept their grades up and their dresses down, and of course, we didn't talk about physical intimacy. Of all the sins you could commit, I was somehow convinced that sex was the ultimate one. So at 18, I was still a virgin. But as my romance with Trevor progressed—and as I started suspecting that I might be one of the few among my classmates who hadn't yet experienced sex—I began thinking about what it would feel like to do it with my boyfriend. At long last, I wanted to know what I'd been missing out on. What was everybody talking about? Trevor seemed like a nice enough guy to show me—and in the summer before I enrolled in college, I decided he was a safe bet. I still wasn't sure when it would happen—but one summer evening as our kisses grew deeper, it finally did. I concluded that sex was overrated. Highly.

Afterward, Trevor was a perfect gentleman—he called and even gave me flowers the next day. We waited a few weeks before we tried it again, and with each attempt, I became more comfortable with physical intimacy and even began to enjoy it. But that pleasure came at a price. First of all, I felt as guilty as I thought I would—and then some. I thought, *Will God send me straight to hell for sleeping with a man who wasn't my husband?* And that leads me to the second point: Since I'd been taught that sex and marriage go hand in hand, I really believed that I should at least consider marrying Trevor simply because we were having sex. Don't get me wrong: I liked him as a boyfriend. Yet I wasn't even close to wanting to exchange vows with him. So when he brought up the topic of a lifelong commitment, I was pretty torn. "What do you think about us getting married?" he asked. I paused. "Well," I said, "I really want to be a singer. How can I be a singer with a husband and kids?" That wasn't exactly the response he was hoping to hear—but it was the only way I could think of to hold him off. Part of me was flattered that he was even asking: Many girls dream of getting such a proposal. And though I'd once fantasized about marrying and settling down, by this point, I was very focused on one thing—finding my way to the stage.

Meanwhile, I suspected that Mom had figured out that Trevor and I were sleeping together. "You can always tell when two people is having sex because they got a darn attitude," she'd often say when I was in earshot. That was as close as Mom ever came to directly addressing what I'm sure she knew was happening.

One Sunday after church, my parents, Trevor, his parents, and I all went out to eat together at a buffet restaurant in Glen Burnie. Toward the end of dinner, just as I was about to raise a spoonful of rice to my mouth, Trevor looked over in the direction of my parents and said something in passing like, "Because you know, I was thinking that Toni and I would get married." My parents froze. "Toni's too young for marriage," Mommy finally said. I shifted a bit in my seat and eventually excused myself to go to the ladies' room. I couldn't believe he'd actually broached the topic with my family. Talk about an awkward way to end dinner.

That evening, I chose to ride back to Severn with my parents rather than with Trevor. In the car on the way home, Dad didn't talk much. Mom, on the other hand, said plenty. "I don't understand why people think that just because you're having sex, you've gotta get married," she muttered. That's when I had my big Aha moment: *I don't have to get married to him—even my mother doesn't think so.* That settled the topic in my mind.

After that night, Trevor never again brought up the subject of marriage. And the more I talked about making it as a professional singer, the further we seemed to drift apart. Our relationship eventually ended, and I can't exactly say I was heartbroken because I was never really in love with him in the first place. But if you're just going to lose your virginity to someone, you could do far worse than Trevor. One pretty decent guy—and for me, one giant step toward womanhood.

I ALWAYS KNEW I'd go to college—my father is a graduate of Bowie State, and my parents both value education. But what I didn't expect was to see Mommy sitting right there in the classroom with me. That's right: My mother went to college the same year I did—during my first two semesters, she signed up for classes so that she could work toward her undergraduate degree.

I took a full course load, and Mommy was in three of my courses: "Intro to Psychology," "Intro to Sociology," and aerobics. I'm like, "Are you kidding me—my mother is taking gym class with me, too?" On Mondays, Wednesdays, and Fridays—the days when our shared courses were scheduled—occasionally, I even had to let her ride to school with me. "There's no use in spending extra gas money," she said. I'd sometimes sit on the other side of the classroom because I felt uncomfortable having my mother so close. Then again, my whole childhood was the perfect training for how to get comfortable with being uncomfortable. "I understand you're embarrassed to be seen with your mom," my father scolded me one day. From then on, I always sat in the desk right next to Mom's.

When I wasn't either studying or dodging my parents, I was rehearsing. My sisters and I were trying to get a gospel album deal, so my parents had us auditioning all over the place. I wasn't the lead singer—Trina was. The tone of her voice was beautiful. We performed everywhere, including at the Kentucky Fried Chicken Gospel Music Competition. We entered the contest four years in a row, and during the final year, we wore matching purple and green neon outfits. Though I wasn't the lead singer (we each had at least one solo), I did lead two songs—"God Is" and "I Know It Was the Blood." Trina sang "Uncloudy Day" by Myrna Summers (and by the way, Trina actually did a duet of that song with Myrna years later). Tamar's solo was "One Day at a Time," the Kris Kristofferson country song that we changed into a gospel style. Because that song contained the lyrics "I'm just a woman," Mommy made Tamar change it to "I'm just a child." "There are no darn women over here!" Mommy told us. We never won the competition—but in our last year, we did make it as far as the semifinals.

Around Maryland, I also sang on my own. I entered a local competition for a chance to perform at the Apollo Theater's Amateur Night in Harlem. I learned a big lesson that night: You've got to know your audience. In the finals, I sang "At This Moment." I'd fallen in love with the song (by Billy Vera and the Beaters) when it was played during a love scene with Michael J. Fox and Tracy Pollan on *Family Ties.* The song might've sounded like a hit on a sitcom episode, but it flopped with a crowd of black folks! I should've chosen an R&B number. The second lesson I learned was this one: Winning is sometimes less about being talented and more about bringing along enough people who can cheer loudly when your name is called. You guessed it—I lost.

I grabbed every opportunity that I could to sing. Between classes, I earned extra money by performing at nightclubs, at fashion shows, at weddings, in competitions. The back of my Honda looked like a suitcase: I packed it with all kinds of dresses and heels, so I could quickly change into the right outfit if somebody called me for a gig at the last minute. In the backseat, I had my Anita Baker outfit (a black dress that I paired with a gold chain and a big belt) and my Spanx-tight "Do Me, Baby" booty dress (the eighties version of an Hervé Léger knockoff, which I wore with stilettos to make me look tall—hey, you've gotta dress for your audience). On Thursday, Friday, and Saturday nights, I did gigs on my own. Every Sunday, I sang with my sisters or played piano for the church choir—yep, I did that, too. I got paid $25 a month for that—$5 a week for the months with five Sundays, and $6.25 a week for the months with just four.

Around town, I became known as the girl who sounded like Anita Baker. In fact, if Anita was coming to our area for a concert but couldn't visit a radio station to do her own promos, DJs like Randy Dennis from V103 in Baltimore would call me in to record the first line of "Sweet Love," Anita Baker's 1986 hit. I made $50 here and there singing jingles and lead-ins for Anita, and people really believed that I was her. I also hustled up any chance I could to be seen or heard: I was even that person who always tried to be the third caller when a radio station hosted a competition. "If people could just hear my voice, I might get discovered," I kept saying to myself. I was doing my own social networking long before anyone had ever heard of Facebook or Twitter. I was always ready to perform: I would sing at the opening of a Band-Aid.

I also held down a thousand other jobs—that's how I scraped together money for my tuition. For a short time, I worked as a court reporter. During another semester, I became a telemarketer. Later, I was an assistant at a finance company.

And if you think that sounds like a lot of skipping around, there's more: I first majored in sociology, then in psych, and finally, at Bowie, in music and in elementary education. At one point, I even thought I wanted to be a pharmacist.

I also transferred a lot. Once I finished a couple semesters at the community college, I enrolled at Morgan State. I then went on to Fleet Business School. My last stop was Bowie State. The truth is that I didn't really want to be a college student at all—I wanted to be a student of music. That's one big reason I moved around so much.

At one of the colleges I attended, I took a job (yes, another one!) in the dean's office. A couple of my friends, Penny and Jackie, worked in the same office with me. One of the guys who worked there always brought in Chinese food, so one afternoon when there wasn't much to do, we all sat around talking and eating. The assistant dean walked in and started chatting with me. "Why do you want to be a singer?" she asked. Everyone knew I was an aspiring musician. "The chances are one in eight million. You should continue your education." I stared at her but didn't respond—I didn't dare say anything back because she was the assistant dean.

I'm sure that woman meant well—but she had no idea just how much passion I had for music. Every time I performed, I felt an immeasurable sense of peace and assurance. In a world in which I could control little else, the one thing I could control was how I expressed myself through song.

From the moment I sang my first solo in church, I felt liberated. I'd often been told that I would never be the lead singer because my voice was too androgynous at a time when soprano soloists were celebrated; I also didn't have a wide vocal range—damn near contralto and on the brink of baritone. "You're more of a background singer," people would often tell me. Even in my family, I was the arranger and the pianist. Trina usually took the lead.

And yet what others said about my voice didn't change my desire to be out front—if anything, their words deepened my resolve to be a soloist and increased my love for music. In a way, I didn't choose music; music chose me. So why did I want to be a singer? Because even with odds that sounded so impossible to my assistant dean, I really couldn't imagine myself doing anything else.

"DAD, CAN I borrow a few bucks?" On a Tuesday morning in 1987, I was trying to round up some gas money to get to my class at Fleet Business School in Annapolis, Maryland. My father handed me a $5 bill, and less than a minute later, I was out the front door of our house and revving up the engine of my Honda. I had just enough cash to make it through the day—$2 for lunch, $3 for gas.

I always got my gas at Amoco. It was the closest to my school and the cheapest I could find—when you're a broke student, every quarter counts. The gas station was on the opposite side of the street from Fleet, so I had to take a slightly different route on the days when I wanted to buy fuel. When I pulled into the lot, I drove onto the full-service side. In those days, when you went over a little bump on the full-service side, a bell rang *(ding, ding!)* to alert an attendant. Once I realized that the full-service gas was twelve cents more per gallon, I pulled out and reparked on the self-service side. I then lifted the nozzle for the unleaded and started pumping. Out of the corner of my eye, I noticed an attendant wearing a blue jumpsuit—he'd heard the bell I'd mistakenly rung the moment before. The man walked toward me.

"Hi, how are you?" he asked, flashing a huge grin. I spotted his under-bite.

"Um, I'm fine," I said while thinking, *Is this man trying to hit on me?* He was short, stout, and African-American, and he looked a few years older than me. The way he swayed his head as he spoke made me want to snicker. Yet in spite of his onesie zip-up and his weird approach, I decided to let him keep talking to me.

"Are you a singer?" he asked.

I stared and pushed the nozzle farther into my tank. "Yes, I am," I said with a confidence that bordered on arrogance. That day, I was rocking a Madonna look: a loose shirt hanging off my right shoulder, a taupe skirt, a row of black rubber bracelets on my arm, and a wide belt slung low toward my left hip. I'd even dipped the ends of my hair in ash-blond dye. Very eighties.

"I'm Bill Pettaway, and I'm a producer," he said, explaining that his job as a gas attendant was his day job. "I've seen you singing around town, and I'd love for you to come to my house and sing some songs. Will you call me?"

I paused. "Okay," I finally said. He then pulled out his card, scribbled a phone number on the back, and handed it to me. I took it.

"You should really call me," he said, probably sensing my hesitation. "I'd really love to work with you." I nodded, thanked him, and then stuffed the paper down in my purse. I was already late for class.

That evening, I called my friend Kim. "I don't think I'm going to call him," I said. "I can't just go over to some strange man's house. I don't even know him. He might be a murderer." Kim disagreed. "Let's go together!" she said. When we were kids, Kim had always been more of a dancer than a singer; to be honest, I hadn't ever really known she wanted to be a singer until the night when I competed in a singing competition at a club, and she said she wanted to compete. She could carry a tune—and by the time I met Bill, she was hoping for a musical break, too. Though I wasn't 100 percent sold on the idea of calling Bill, I did sense that his energy was good. My gut told me he was okay. "We should just try it!" Kim said.

In today's world, a wannabe singer probably wouldn't just run into an up-and-coming producer at a gas station. But during the late eighties and early nineties, that wasn't quite as unlikely as it sounds. Dozens of producers like Bill who were trying to make it in the business were more plentiful— especially since this was all long before the days when any would-be artists could just put themselves out there on YouTube and hope to get noticed. Back then, a new singer needed a liaison. And it just so happened that in my area of the country, some big names like Johnny Gill and the group Star-point, Tony Terry, and Chuck Brown had been discovered. That might've been why talent scouts were popping up. But while running into Bill might've been more probable then than it would be now, let me be clear about one thing: It was nothing short of a miracle that he happened to spot me that day and ac-tually recognize me as someone he'd seen performing around town. A moment like that usually only rolls around once in a girl's life—and this was my big opportunity. And even as I de-cided whether I should call Bill, I somehow knew that.

By the next afternoon, I'd decided to take the risk and call Bill. I fished out the crumpled piece of paper from my purse and dialed Bill's number. He answered after two rings.

"Hello," he said.

"Hi, how are you?"

"Who's this?"

"This is Toni," I answered. "We met at the gas station the other day."

"Oh yes—I remember," he said. "I'm so glad you called."

"I would love to come over and do some demos," I said. "My friend Kim is coming with me. Where do you live?"

"I'm in Annapolis," he said. He then gave me his address and we agreed to meet at seven the following evening.

When Kim and I knocked on the front door, an older woman answered. It was Bill's mother—and she looked like the female version of him. I was relieved that his mother lived there; that probably meant he wasn't a murderer. "Come on in," she said, as if she'd been expecting us. We stepped into the foyer. "Bill, your guests are here!" she yelled out. A couple minutes later, Bill greeted us, then led us down a set of steep stairs toward his makeshift studio. For some reason, I imagined that Bill's studio would be huge—but as it turns out, it was in his mama's finished basement. The walls were soundproofed with a material that looked like egg crates.

Like most men, Bill couldn't keep his eyes off my friend Kim—she has gorgeous brown skin and a magnificent smile. I was so used to her being hot and my being homey, which is why Bill's gawking didn't bother me. It was the classic *Beaches* story: CC, Bette Midler's character, wanted to be a star singer, but everyone was always looking at her best friend, Hillary (played by Barbara Hershey). I may not have been all that confident about my appearance, but I was sure about one thing: I could sing.

"Let me play you a couple of tracks," Bill said, keeping his gaze fixed on Kim. He then played a song that he'd written for one of the guys in Starpoint, the R&B group. "How do you like the song?" We both nodded. "I've also done some stuff for Milli Vanilli," he said, explaining that he'd cowritten "Girl You Know It's True." At the time, the world hadn't even yet heard of Milli Vanilli or the song that made them famous, but Kim and I were nonetheless impressed that Bill had actually worked with a professional artist. As we chatted, I could feel a set of goose bumps forming on the back of my neck. *Bill is a real producer,* I thought. *This could be my magical moment.* After listening to a couple more tracks, we thanked Bill and he escorted us to the front door. Once Kim and I were back inside my Honda, we hugged each other and squealed. "I think this is the real thing, girl!" I said. "It sure feels like it!" Kim said in agreement.

Our first visit to the studio was just a listening session for us to see if we liked Bill's music—that's usually the way it goes. The plan was for me to create a demo that Bill could shop around. So a week later, we returned for a second visit. This time when we arrived at Bill's place, Ky Adeyemo—one of the guys from Starpoint—was in the studio. Ky and Bill had cowritten a song called "Maybe Baby." Bill played the song for us, and I listened closely to the girl's voice on the track. "How about if you try it now?" said Bill, handing me a sheet with the lyrics. I nodded and took the sheet. "Maybe baby, you were in love with me," I began. I didn't feel even a tinge of nervousness—probably because I'd been performing for most of my life. Once I finished the song, Kim gave it a try as well. She was good—but I knew I'd outsung her.

After the session, Bill walked us back to the front door. "Wow, you can really sing!" he turned to me and said. "You sound like Anita Baker." No shock there.

Back at home, I finally worked up the nerve to tell my parents that I'd met with Bill and even gone to his house—and surprisingly, they didn't overreact. That's mostly because they remembered meeting Bill's parents at a church conference.

In between classes, I met with Bill whenever I could. My friend Kim eventually moved to Europe, so Bill began working with me one-on-one. As we recorded one song at a time for the demo, he talked me up to the musicians he knew. He finally mentioned me to Ernesto Phillips—the lead singer for Starpoint. Ernesto also had his own production company, Elektra. "I heard about that girl," Ernesto said when Bill told him about my demo. "Let me check her out," he said. After Bill played him a couple songs from my demo, Ernesto said he wanted to hear me sing in person. "Really?!" I said when Bill gave me that news. "That's right," Bill said. "He wants you to come meet him in his studio." I nearly passed out. It's one thing to randomly bump into a producer at a gas station—but it's a whole different thing to connect with the lead singer of one of the hottest groups. Later that night before I went to sleep, I literally got down on my knees and prayed. "God," I whispered, "please let me become a famous singer." Years later, I'd come to realize that I should've been far more specific with my request.

The next week, I drove to Ernesto's home in Crofton, Maryland—his studio was on the top floor of his three-level town house. "How are you?" he said to me at the front door. "I'm great," I answered, hoping he wouldn't notice the sweat that had formed at my temples. In the studio, he asked me to sing a song that he'd written. To this day, I can't recall what that song was—and that's probably because I was so anxious. But apparently he liked what he heard: After just that one session, he said, "I'd love to sign you." I was ecstatic.

To this day, I'm still shocked that it all happened the way it did—and so fast. Who knew that a trip to a gas station would lead me to the doorstep of a different life? It has been said that there are just six degrees of separation between every person on the planet—but in this case, it seemed there were only three. Even with all of the talent scouts and producers working in the Maryland and D.C. area, no human could have predicted that Bill, Ernesto, and I would cross paths. That's exactly why I believe it was a God thing.

I finally mentioned my meeting with Ernesto to Mommy. She and Dad asked me a thousand questions, of course, but they were happy about the opportunity—this was as close to fame as I'd ever gotten. When my parents realized that Ernesto's father, George Phillips, was a chief of psychiatry at Crownsville Hospital, that put them even more at ease. Plus, my father had met Dr. Phillips while visiting churches. So by the time Ernesto came by to meet my parents and the rest of the family, Mommy and Daddy were already convinced he was legit.

Soon after Ernesto signed me, we began strategizing. "How do you see yourself onstage?" he asked. "Do you know what you'll wear? And who will your background singers be?"

"I'll have my sisters do my background," I said.

"Those little girls?" He seemed surprised.

"Yes," I said.

He paused and then repeated himself: "Those little girls—they can sing that well?"

I nodded. "You have to come hear them."

A couple weeks later, my sisters and I gathered in our living room and sang "If You're Happy and You Know It." By the look on Ernesto's face, we knew he was impressed with our masterful pitch and intricate five-part harmony. "This is a gold mine!" he said, looking over at my parents. "I can't believe this is untapped. I haven't heard talent like this since the Jackson Five. I could sign all of you guys tomorrow!"

The next morning, that's exactly what he did. In the summer of 1988, my sisters and I landed our very first deal.

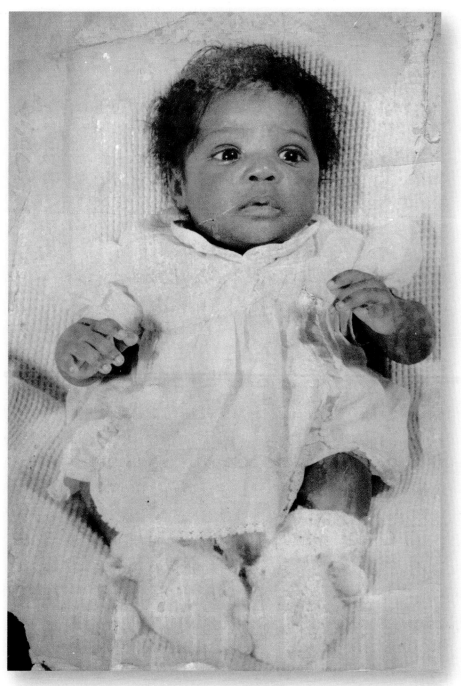

One of my first baby pictures, at three months old.

Our childhood home in Severn, Maryland. Every year in the spring, Mommy would paint the big rock (there in the yard) with "The Braxton Family." She changed the paint color each year.

An early school photo—I was five years old here.

Enjoying ice cream in the summer with Mommy at Grandma Eva's house in Baltimore.

Family photo from the late 1980s—I'm standing in the back, second from the left.

All dressed up and posing in front of our house before heading to church on Easter Sunday.

All of the siblings together at Grandma Eva's house on Easter Sunday.

At age sixteen, I was already practicing how to look like a star.

With my senior prom date, Ferron, when he came to pick me up from my house.

This picture is from my senior
year in high school. Note my
monogrammed sweater!

My sisters and I
performed at Anne
Orundel Community
College in Arnold,
Maryland. I played piano
for the group and sang a
solo of the gospel song
"God Is."

All smiles at my graduation
from Glen Burnie High School
in Glen Burnie, Maryland.

I wore this outfit when my sisters and I performed a showcase for L.A. Reid and Babyface in Atlanta shortly before I signed with LaFace Records. I was about twenty-three years old here.

Performing as the Braxton Sisters at Bowie State University in Maryland.
I'm right in the middle!

A signed promo shot from the Braxton Sisters'
single, "The Good Life." This is the only single all
five of us ever released as a family group.

(©Robert Manella for Atlantic Records)

In 1995, LaFace Records hosted a party for me, their new artist, and my family drove up from Maryland to take part in the festivities.

(courtesy of Anita and Steve Shevett)

My sisters (Trina, Traci, Tamar, and Towanda) joined me for a European tour on the heels of the success of my 1996 *Secrets* album.

I was honored to be cast as the first African American woman to play a leading role in a Disney production on Broadway when I starred as Belle in *Beauty and the Beast*. This was our cast bow at the show's final performance.

(courtesy of Anita and Steve Shevett, used with permission from Disney)

A promotional postcard used to advertise my Broadway role in *Beauty and the Beast*.
(©Disney. Photography by Lynn Goldsmith)

I was thrilled to return to Broadway to play the title role in *Aida*. I love this Times Square shot of my two Broadway billboards side by side!
(used with permission from Disney)

April 22, 2001, one of the happiest days of my life: my wedding to Keri Lewis at Dean Gardens in Atlanta, Georgia. *(©Yitzhak Dalal)*

Proudly showing off my baby bump with Keri—this was during my pregnancy with our first son, Denim Cole Braxton-Lewis, born December 2, 2001. *(©Daniela Federici)*

This was our number in Vegas for "7 Whole Days." I am definitely not a dancer by nature—the color of your skin doesn't always mean you have rhythm! We practiced for six weeks, and my dancers and their amazing bodies were my inspiration. (© Keirston "Keri" Lewis)

We almost had a wardrobe malfunction with this Vegas costume—as you can see, it was cut pretty high. Let's just say I was very glad I had just been lasered!

(© Keirston "Keri" Lewis)

Here I'm singing "Un-break My Heart"—we were trying to re-create the video onstage in this white dress. This has become the song that I'm most known for, which is why I wanted to make it the title of my book.

(© Keirston "Keri" Lewis)

CHAPTER 7

Good Life

How do you write songs for a group of girls whose ages span a decade? That's the big question that arose for Ernesto once he welcomed us onto his label. In 1988, I was a twenty-one-year-old with a mature voice that was as thick as a milk shake—and little Tamar, just eleven then, still had the high-pitched vocal range of a preadolescent. "Maybe Toni could be the lead singer," Ernesto said to my parents—but Mommy shot down that idea. "Toni is not the Braxtons," she retorted. "This is an ensemble." Ernesto's concern was that he wouldn't be able to market us. Yes, he'd signed us to his production company, but his grand plan was to create our demo and then shop us around to the major record companies. That's hard to do with a group that includes both a tween and a twentysomething.

Once we signed with Ernesto, I got my first lesson in the music business: You earn peanuts in the beginning. My mother hired a local two-bit attorney who oversaw our deal. We received $5,000 in total: $2,500 as a signing bonus, and $2,500 on the back end, once the demo was finished. We also agreed to 50 percent of any future profits—and Ernesto would get the other half. He'd use part of those profits to cover the expenses he'd incur while preparing our demo. Producers know that they don't have to negotiate with an unknown artist who's hungry for success. You either agree to the deal or you lose your chance to break in.

Ernesto did his best to write music that could include all of our voices. On the weekends, we began recording songs at Starpoint's studio. One song he came up with was a remake of the sixties hit "When Something Is Wrong with My Baby." My parents objected. "My eleven-year-old child ain't singing 'When something's wrong with my baby,' " Mommy said. "She should be singing about her baby doll, not her baby." Ernesto was stumped—he didn't know how to respond to my mother. When he and I talked privately, he'd tell me, "Your mother's a tough cookie. I've gotta find a way to work this out." In the following months, he'd repeat that just about every week. Even still, Ernesto stuck with us; I think he really liked us. And as he spent more time with our family, he became more and more emotionally invested.

By the time we started working with Ernesto, I was pretty

used to my parents' strong opinions. But I didn't challenge them—in our family and community, you just didn't do that. Parents were the ultimate authority, and children were to do as they were told. In my head, I'd be thinking, *Why can't Tamar sing "When Something Is Wrong With My Baby?"* But every time my parents challenged Ernesto about our musical selections, I simply did what I'd always done: I stood by and quietly listened. Were there times when I wished we could have hired an outside manager, so that my parents could just be my parents? Absolutely. But whatever I might've felt, I knew better than to vocalize it. And besides that, even when I didn't agree with my parents or like their approach, I believed their intentions were good.

From the start, Ernesto molded us as artists. "You need to go see concerts," he told us. He wanted us to become familiar with the business by studying other musicians. So one weekend, my sisters and I went to the Budweiser Superfest, which featured Al B. Sure, New Edition, and Bobby Brown. During an intermission, Ernesto took me backstage to meet a few people. While I was back there, one of the show's producers spotted me and said, "Hey, let's use her!"—they'd planned for Bobby Brown to bring some girl up onto the stage during the second half of the concert. So along with another girl who was chosen, I waited in the wings until Bobby called me out onstage. "Little shorty right there, come on over," he said, beckoning. He started singing into the mic—"The truth about Roni . . ."—and I started trying to sing with him! I think Bobby was surprised that I was actually more interested in singing than in shrieking. After all, the whole idea of calling a girl up onstage is so that she can scream and faint. Once the song was finished, Bobby goes, "Damn, she's skinny!" The crowd erupted in laughter. I just stood there and blushed. I could feel my oversized hot-pink sweater sliding off my right shoulder. "Are you one of them salad-eating bitches?" he asked, stealing a line from Eddie Murphy's comedy show *Raw.* "No," I said, "I like to eat!" After my two minutes of fame, I returned to my seat next to my sisters in the audience. We all high-fived. "That was great!" Traci told me.

Even when you know how to sing, you have to be trained. There's a big difference between singing a song in church and delivering a professional performance. That's why Ernesto and his colleagues spent so much time refining our raw talent. Renée Diggs, a singer in Starpoint, taught me how to control my vibrato. She and Ernesto also showed me how to infuse my songs with emotion. "The idea is to engage your audience," Ernesto explained. "You always want to make them want more." I learned how to speed up or slow down at various points in a song, and how to go tender or aggressive. I'll always be grateful that Ernesto taught me far more than just how to sing. He taught me how to create a musical story—full of peaks and valleys—that moves every person in the audience.

As we prepared our demo, Ernesto never declared me the lead singer of the Braxtons—but he did give me the most powerful parts of the songs. "Good Life" was our first single, and my voice is featured prominently throughout. Once we'd completed the vocals, Ernesto came to our church and recorded my dad's prayer and inserted it into the song; Kevin Liles, who was in the group Numarx, added a rap. Mommy was pretty happy with how the song turned out, mostly because the lyrics were clean. She'd already given Ernesto her edict: "You're not gonna have my children singing 'bout no booties or behinds"—which is why we ended up singing generic, honey-filled songs. We were singing Creed-style songs long before that band even existed.

Once we completed our "Good Life" demo, Ernesto rushed it off to his contacts at Warner Bros. Records (which was Madonna's label back then . . . I studied which artists were on which labels!) and Arista Records. Ernesto already had a relationship with Arista because of Starpoint's connection with Milli Vanilli, who'd signed with the label—and it was because of Ernesto's connection that our demo even got heard. I don't recall whether Ernesto ever told us about the record company execs' initial response to our demo—but it must have been decent, because we were invited on a short trip to New York City. In Manhattan, we would meet with various record execs and let them hear us sing. I'd later realize that this was all part of the schmoozing game that happens in the music business: The record companies bring a new artist to their offices, they get you all excited about the possibility of signing with the label, and then they later try to sign you for pennies, nickels, and dimes. But we'll get to that part later.

My sisters and I, along with our mother and dad, boarded

an Amtrak to New York City (we were scared to fly and even used a leisure van to get around to our church concerts in Maryland . . . very country suburban). We checked into an inexpensive hotel and divided up into three rooms. For dinner, we ordered from the room service menu—I had the chicken wings, which were around $7.99, and my sisters each made their selection. When we got the final bill, my jaw nearly hit the floor—the gratuity and delivery charges made the whole bill more than $100! Who knew room service could add up to so much? Certainly not a group of girls from Severn.

That night, I was so excited I could barely sleep. Just being in New York made me feel like I'd already made it: the bright lights, the bustling sidewalks, the millions of people who seemed to carry ambitions as big as mine. I'd always wanted to be famous—and it seemed like I was on the doorstep of that dream. Whenever I found myself fantasizing about a singing career, I pictured myself up on a stage. Yes, I'd been singing with my sisters for all of my life but in my heart of hearts, I always knew I wanted to be a soloist.

The next morning, our first stop was Arista. When we walked up to the granite building, I looked up and eyed the gold capital letters—ARISTA. Seeing the logo made me feel like I was already a star. Inside, the halls were lined with photos of famous Arista singers. Dionne Warwick. Whitney Houston. Barry Manilow. The security guard at the front desk handed each of us a name badge, and we stepped onto the elevator. Upstairs, we met Erik Nuri, an A&R guy. Erik trotted us around to various departments, like publicity and sales, just to say hello and let everyone have a look at us. We eventually rounded the corner of the hallway that led to the office of Arista's founder, Clive Davis. At the time, he was already a legend in the record business, and he was best known for having launched the careers of some of the industry's brightest stars—like Aretha Franklin; Aerosmith; Earth, Wind & Fire; and, of course, Whitney. "Let's see if he has time to say hello," said the man. Clive was just finishing up a call and was on his way out and gave us a quick hello. The whole exchange was less than a minute—Clive hadn't been scheduled to meet us, yet he was just gracious enough to make time to say hi because we were passing through. Almost as soon as he'd greeted us, we were on our way back down the hall.

At Warner Bros., we met with Benny Medina—the celebrated record executive who'd once written for the Temptations, Smokey Robinson, and Rick James. That day, we'd all worn the same curly hairstyle—except for Tamar, who had bangs and a ponytail. "So why is your hair different?" he joked with Tamar. I could tell that he liked Tamar's feisty personality (yes, she was as feisty at eleven as she is now!). Benny also recognized that we had talent: "You girls can sing," he said as we were leaving. But in my gut, I had the feeling that we wouldn't end up on his label.

I was right. A few weeks after we returned to Severn, Ernesto stopped by our house with some news: "Arista wants to sign you!" he told us. In the fall of 1989, we got a singles deal for "The Good Life." For me, "the great life" seemed like a far more accurate description.

. . .

MOST ENTERTAINERS GO through a process called artist development—which involves defining your image through hairstyle and fashion. In Berry Gordy's early years at Motown, for instance, he was known for investing in his singers' public profiles. Now it was our turn: Once Arista signed us, we returned to New York for our makeovers. Our exhilaration about revisiting the big city (we'd never seen so many skyscrapers in our lives!) was soon replaced with another emotion—disappointment. In short, our makeovers were awful.

Since we were unproven artists with only a singles deal, we didn't exactly get the five-star treatment. Our stylist was awful: She blow-dried my baby-fine hair and sewed in two or three rows of weave tracks to give me some volume. But the tracks were way too tight (ouch!), and later, during our promotional photos, I stripped them out and just pulled my hair into a ponytail. Towanda got curly hair extensions; Traci wore her hair tapered in the back (very MC Lyte), which was her favorite look in the eighties; and the stylist didn't do anything to Tamar's or Trina's hair (they both already had long, thick manes . . . especially Trina). As for makeup, the artist made me about two shades darker than I am. And I could actually see the line between my dark face and my light neck! It was a disaster.

In those days, nothing happened fast in the music business. Even once you land a record deal, it's as if your project is put onto a conveyor belt—and you have to wait your turn for your new music to be released. So we couldn't just say, "Here's our single—go ahead and release it." We had to be slotted in. That's why an entire year passed between inking a deal and having our song introduced to the world.

Back in Severn, my day-to-day life didn't change much. By 1989, I was a student at Bowie State University. I'd finally moved out of my parents' house and begun sharing an apartment near campus with Jackie and Penny. My friends were all ahead of me in completing their education: I'd transferred around so much (and lost credits along the way!) that I was starting my junior year; they were all working on their master's degrees. Even still, we were all like peas and carrots—practically inseparable.

I started dating a Georgetown med-school student—and I'll spare him the embarrassment of revealing his name. His family (which included three generations of wealthy dentists) wasn't into the arts, which is why he had an issue with my pursuing a music career. "You should be taking a heavier course load," he'd often say. He was in his residency and about to become an anesthesiologist. "Why don't you finish school?" In addition to being unsupportive of my dream, he was also somewhat of an egomaniac: "You and I are probably going to marry," he said, "and any woman who wants to become my wife has to sign a prenup." I was excited about his semi-proposal, but I was completely over the idea of being the wife of a powerful man. I wanted to be my own woman—and to have my own voice.

On Tuesday, September 4, 1990—a full year after Arista signed us—our song finally hit the radio airwaves. Leading up to the debut, I'd told all my friends and classmates to turn their dials to 95.5 WPGC, an FM station in Maryland. I knew exactly which window of time the song would be played in—the record company had told us that. I hopped into my Honda (and yes, all my performance outfits were still spilling out of the back!) and I began my drive to school. Just as I pulled into the parking lot, "Summertime"—the DJ Jazzy Jeff and the Fresh Prince hit, which was one of the biggest songs of the year—began playing. I sang along. As the song's last notes faded, the announcer introduced us: "And up next," he said, "we've got Maryland's own . . . the Braxtons!" My pulse sped up. I put the car in park, turned off the engine, and turned up the radio. At last, I heard the opening line I'd practiced so many times: "When will people ever learn . . . wonder will they ever turn!"

The song wasn't a hit—and I knew that right away. How did I know? Because it just didn't seem to fit with the other popular songs on the radio. It didn't blend well. The first time I heard "Summertime," for instance, I could tell you that it would become a hit—I knew that at hello. The rhythm, the lyrics, the way it reverberated in my Honda—I could just feel that it would resonate. Have you ever heard a song and then wondered, *Why in the world did they put that out?* It's sometimes because the artist and the producers have made the mistake of only listening to a song on the big speakers in the studio—and every song sounds like a hit on those speakers. But when you've truly got a hit, it sounds like one even through a car's small radio speakers. From the opening note to the closing refrain, our song simply didn't have the sound of a chart-topper. Period. But that didn't make me any less proud. Whatever happened, we had a single out—and the excitement of that just smacked the piss out of me and my sisters.

Later that day, Ernesto and I caught up by phone. "How did it sound?" he asked.

"It was all right," I said.

Noticing my obvious lack of enthusiasm, he pressed on: "Well what song did it follow?"

" 'Summertime,' " I responded.

"Well nothing would sound like a hit after *that* song!" he said. "That's the biggest hit of the year! I'm sure it'll do great. You'll see."

Soon after, my sisters and I set out on a three-week tour to promote the single. Do you have any idea what it's like to show up at a nightclub and sing a song that contains the Lord's Prayer? The crowd would be listening to house music or something, and then we'd march in with our Christian inspirational number. At Zanzibar in midtown Manhattan, we actually got booed! One lady in the audience said, "Don't boo them—they can sing," but that didn't erase my embarrassment. At a few other stops, we did get some claps from the audience; we also got encouragement from Bubba, a singer in the R&B group Today. "You guys are so talented," he said when he met us. During our eight gigs on the road, we also did a little press: Cynthia Horner from *Right On!* magazine interviewed us. As the eldest, I did most of the talking. She asked me all about what it was like to grow up as a preacher's kid and then transition to a singing career. I was so thrilled just to be talking to her that I can't really remember what I said—but I did plenty of smiling and gushing. I felt honored to be talking with anyone from *Right On!*—whenever I'd get my copy back when I was a kid, I'd pull out the centerfold posters of artists like Michael Jackson and New Edition and hang them in my closet.

It didn't take long for us to realize that "Good Life" was doing badly. Don't get me wrong: We could've done much worse than number 79 on the *Billboard* charts. But when Clive and his execs took note of our single's weak performance, he began to ask himself the same question that Ernesto had been asking: How do I package these girls? That's when he made a phone call that would become pivotal for us.

In January 1990, Clive dialed up Antonio "L.A." Reid and Kenneth "Babyface" Edmonds—the powerhouse producers whose company, LaFace Records, was still a brand-new label under Arista. "We've got these girls," Clive told them. "And to be honest, I just don't know what to do with them. You've gotta take a look." L.A. and Kenny weren't all that interested. That was mostly because they'd just signed TLC, the R&B trio discovered by Pebbles Reid, who was then L.A.'s wife.

But Clive insisted that they hear us perform. "Just let them do one showcase for you," he said, pressing them. "They can fly down to Atlanta."

Reluctantly, L.A. and Kenny agreed to take the meeting. No one could've predicted the painful episode that would follow: Five bright-eyed Braxton sisters would soon be narrowed down to one.

CHAPTER 8

Going Solo

Y ou already know that I chose to take the solo deal with
L.A. and Kenny despite my mother's explosion. Now
here's the second half of that story: Even a couple days after
our Braxton Family Civil War, my parents still seemed pissed.
Very. But undeterred by their reaction (and quite frankly, still
in shock that they'd turned on me in the first place), I packed a
bag and headed off. "Kenny wants you to go to Dayton, Ohio,
for a couple weeks to work with Midnight Star," my manager,
Greg, had told me. Kenny had some kind of production deal
with that R&B group, and the idea was to send me to them for
a studio recording boot camp. I probably would've hightailed
it to the moon if Kenny had asked me to. This was the man
whose records I had listened to for hours on end—from the

first note to the last yodel. I was pretty much in wonder of his talent.

I was petrified the first time I showed up at the studio. The soundproofed room was painted in an amber tone, and it was much larger than any studio I'd ever seen. The floors were made of hardwood. In one corner sat a piano and a set of drums; in another area, there was a huge vocal booth—more like its own room than a booth. I walked over to the booth and put on my headphones. A producer played a track for me. The second time he played it, he asked me to sing along. I did.

Right away, I felt like I'd failed. It was clear that the producers wanted me to sing like Midnight Star's lead vocalist, Belinda Lipscomb—but her voice was much higher than mine. "Try it this way," said Bo Watson, one of the members of Midnight Star. He was trying to get me to mimic Belinda's vibrato. But I couldn't make myself sound like her. It took me the whole two weeks to master just a couple of songs—and there was absolutely no magic. By the end of my time there, I had just one thought: *Kenny and L.A. are going to drop me.*

I returned to Maryland feeling deflated. The depression didn't have much time to settle in because I had two weeks to pack up my whole life and get to Atlanta, which is where Kenny and L.A. were based. I guess I hadn't completely blown it in Ohio, because Kenny and L.A. still wanted me to come down and begin recording. Before I said good-bye to my classmates (I'd completed up to my junior year at Bowie State) and headed off to a whole new life, I wanted to change my look. I let a local hairstylist cut my shoulder-length hair into a short style. I just wanted a whole new look to go along with the brand-new life I was beginning. My Honda had died, so my father arranged to get me a Mercedes 190—the car had belonged to my manager, and Dad asked him if I could just take over the payments. My Honda had been $185 a month, and the Mercedes would be like $199.

A friend and I stuffed the Benz with my belongings and made the trip down to Atlanta together. As we slowly backed out of the driveway, the frame dropped a bit with the weight of everything I owned. My hometown—the place where my dream began—grew smaller in the distance with each passing mile. We made our way onto I-85 South and settled in for the ten-hour journey to Georgia. I used my Motorola flip phone to check in with my parents, which I did just about every hour. "Where are you now?" my dad would ask with a touch of panic in his voice. I'm sure he and Mommy were just concerned about my safety on the road. By this time, Mom had started to chill out a little and settle into the idea that I was moving forward. We didn't really talk about the episode, but I could just tell things had simmered down. In spite of the fact that she didn't agree with my choice to take the solo deal, she was still a good mom—and that meant she was nervous about seeing me drive off onto the interstate and begin a big adventure on my own.

I showed up in Atlanta with $300 to my name and plenty of student loan debt. Since I hadn't yet nailed down an apartment, I moved into one of those extended-stay places in Buckhead on Piedmont Road. A woman named Connie from the record company had explained to me that I could move into an apartment that would be paid for out of my artist budget. I didn't quite realize it then, but that meant I was essentially paying for the place myself. Let me explain.

I signed on with LaFace Records as a "singer/songwriter"—which meant I would be paid to perform and write music. L.A. and Kenny were to receive 50 percent of my songwriting royalties through their company, Jay Bird Alley Publishing. In the music business, the record company determines an overall budget for an artist's project—and mine was about $100,000. Of that $100,000, I received a signing bonus of $30,000 that I used to pay off my student loans. That up-front money is like a loan that the record company gives you—but that loan has to be paid back with any profits that you eventually earn.

Here's the part that a lot of people don't understand: A singer's signing bonus, all of her personal expenses, and all of the costs of making the album are deducted from the overall project budget. So if the budget is $100K, and your total expenses add up to $99,000, you're left with a $1,000 paycheck. In short, it might've seemed like the record company was covering my rent—but it was being deducted from the budget. That's why just about every performer starts out in the hole. It's a standard contract that most new artists sign.

A few hours after my friend got me settled into my place and flew back to Severn, L.A. dropped by. "You're here!" he said. "How was the trip?"

"It was fine," I said.

"Let's go over to the studio," he said.

"Now?" I responded. I glanced down at my Levi's and neon-yellow sweatshirt—the one with African kids dancing on the front. "Can I change?" I said.

"You're fine like you are," he said, smiling. So I grabbed my fake Chanel purse (one that I'd bought at TJ Maxx) and hopped into the passenger seat of L.A.'s black Benz.

The studio was at L.A.'s house. As he drove us there, we chatted. "So what kind of music do you see yourself doing?" he asked, trying to get into my head. "Who do you like?"

"I really love Anita," I said.

"Do you think you'd get excited if you met Anita right now?" he asked.

I nodded.

"I promise you that a year from now, you'll be excited but you won't show it," he said with a grin. "You're going to have so many great experiences." We finally pulled up to the gate of his community and a guard let us in. As we talked, I stared out the window to see row after row of enormous homes with immaculately manicured lawns in his country club. We pulled into his driveway.

When I walked through his front door, my jaw hit the ground. The place must've been ten thousand square feet! Stunning oversized artwork lined the walls. A taupe Kreiss sofa sat in the living room. Long, sheer, Mediterranean-style curtains flowed down from their rods and swayed as the breeze blew in. Even the floors were special—pickled hardwood in an off-white color. In college, I had once dated a guy whose place was decorated in a similar way—God only knows where he got the money. I'm grateful that I'd at least had that much exposure, because otherwise, I probably would've lost my mind the first time I saw L.A.'s living room. "Come on in," he told me. "Make yourself at home."

He first took me into the hair salon—yes, he had one of those in his house, too. L.A. was then married to Pebbles, and she owned the production label Pebbitone. Pebbles, whose own 1987 solo album went platinum, had discovered the R&B group TLC; L.A. and Kenny eventually signed them on to LaFace. When we rounded the corner into the salon, I met Tionne "T-Boz" Watkins and Lisa "Left Eye" Lopes from TLC—they weren't yet famous at the time, but they would be later. Debra Jean "Deah Dame" Hurd (of the group Damian Dame, the first act signed to LaFace) and Marie Davis, a hairstylist with Pebbitone, were both there. So was Pebbles. "Nice to meet you!" said Pebbles. I could hardly believe I was standing in the same room with all these famous people—or that I might be on my way to becoming one of them. Unbelievable.

I was in awe of Pebbles. I'd seen beauty like hers on television, but never in person. She was so well manicured and stylish, and she had the most amazing thick hair. As I stood there in my jeans and ugly sweatshirt and clutched my knockoff handbag, I suddenly felt out of place. After a couple minutes of chatting, L.A. and I left the room. As we exited, I heard Pebbles say, "She's country—but she's a cute girl."

L.A. called his recording studio, which was in his guesthouse, LaCoco. We didn't do much in the studio that first day.

L.A. just played a couple demo tracks he'd been working on for Anita Baker; L.A. and Kenny were in final negotiations with Paramount to produce the soundtrack for the Eddie Murphy movie *Boomerang*. So they wanted to have a few songs ready in case the deal came through. The real recording began a couple days later when I met with Kenny. The plan was for me to record the demo of two songs that Kenny was writing for Anita. Anita would eventually listen to that demo to get a feel for the songs.

L.A. represented the business side of LaFace—and Kenny was the creative force. That's probably why I was so starstruck the first day we worked together. Back when I heard Kenny's 1986 record *Lovers,* I went crazy over his voice. I even started trying to yodel the way he did! I thought of myself as the female version of Kenny. I'd often tell my brother, Mikey, "He is going to produce my albums one day"—and here I was, about to live that fantasy.

When I arrived at L.A.'s studio for the second time, Bo Watson (the Midnight Star keyboardist who'd coached me in Dayton) was there. L.A. introduced me to the team in the studio—and I thought the sound engineer looked like John Oates, that curly-haired musician in Hall & Oates. Kenny walked in and greeted me. "Wow, you cut your hair!" he said. "I like it." I blushed a little.

Kenny had been working on the lyrics for the duet "Give U My Heart." Bo began playing the melody and Kenny sang along. After a couple verses, he asked me to join in. A few minutes into our duet, the vocal booth began having some technical difficulties and then it actually broke down. "Let's record it in the bathroom," said Kenny. "The acoustics are great in there." So we stepped into the small space, which was all black with granite walls; a shimmering crystal chandelier hung from above. Over the next hour, we recorded the entire song in there.

In the following days, Kenny and I worked on additional tracks for Anita Baker—"You Mean the World to Me" and "Another Sad Love Song," which was the most beautiful melody I'd ever heard. I sang the demo for both of the songs, though we didn't actually finish "You Mean the World to Me." I was the best artist Kenny and L.A. could've chosen at that time in their careers, because I could be so easily molded. If they told me what to sing, I sang it. I was excited just to be recording a demo for a singer I admired so much—that was my claim to fame. I kept thinking, *I'm the girl who gets to do a demo for Anita Baker.* You couldn't tell me I wasn't already a star.

Completely surreal—that's how I'd describe those first weeks in Atlanta. You know that magical feeling you get the first time you go to Disney World at night, and you see the castle all lit up? That's the feeling I had. I thought I was the luckiest girl in the world. I'd gone from performing in front of my mirror with a ketchup bottle in Severn to singing a duet with a huge star in a blinged-up powder room. If that dream could come true, anything in the world seemed possible.

. . .

IN THOSE DAYS, my whole way of thinking was very green—and it didn't take L.A. and Kenny long to realize that. "You were in college to be a teacher," Kenny said to me one afternoon. "How much does a guy have to make for you to date him?"

Without pausing, I declared, "I would've been making thirty thousand dollars a year as a teacher—so he would have to make thirty-one thousand dollars."

They laughed so hard that they almost fell on the floor. "You're absolutely going to change your mind," Kenny said once he'd recovered from his outburst. "He'll need to make more than that!"

Another time, Kenny mentioned the movie *Star Wars*, his favorite film. "You've seen it, right?" I hadn't. So the next week, he pulled out his laser disc (a bigger version of a DVD) and made me sit for six hours and watch the entire trilogy.

Kenny and L.A. became like brothers to me—and I trusted them fully. We'd joke around in the studio, which is where I spent 99 percent of my time.

"Whatcha doin'?" Kenny would call and ask me.

"Not much," I'd usually say.

"You should come by the studio."

Even if Kenny and I weren't working, I'd just go and observe whatever he was doing. I wanted to learn absolutely everything I could about the music business.

Back then, I had a horrible crush on Kenny. There, I said it: I was smitten. That changed in an instant on the day when I met Tracey, his fiancée—I didn't even know he was engaged!

Tracey was stunningly beautiful, and once I realized Kenny was in the trophy business, I knew I had no shot. Not that Kenny was paying me a bit of attention anyway: He has always seen me as a little sister. That's still true even now.

One day while Kenny and I were in the studio, recording a demo, L.A. swung by. "How many records do you think you'll sell on your first album?" he asked, smiling.

I pondered that for a moment. "I'll go double platinum at least," I said with confidence.

"You think you'll go double platinum?" he said.

I nodded.

"Let's make a deal," he said. "If you go double platinum, I'll buy you any kind of car you want."

Without missing a beat, I told him, "I want a Porsche." He and Kenny exchanged a glance and then chuckled.

I was L.A. and Kenny's little tagalong. If either of them went out shopping, for instance, I'd be like, "Can I go?" I was curious about everything: how they picked their furniture, how they discerned good quality, and what they considered stylish. I was always respectful about giving them their space, yet I still asked a million questions. Especially around the studio, I was privy to a lot of conversations. "We'll do four points on this song," I once heard Kenny say. That's how I discovered that Kenny and L.A. were five-point producers. Each "point" is equal to about 1 percent of the royalty profits that a producer receives on a song, and those points are usually based on the producer's experience and notoriety. The number of points is negotiable: If a record sells one hundred thousand copies, for instance, then the producer's percentage of profits can be bumped up by a half a point or more. It was all a whole new world for me—and like a sponge, I soaked it up.

For a girl who'd just scored a record deal with two of the biggest names in the business, I actually felt very lonely. My friend Kim had stayed in London to take a government job, so we rarely talked. And since I spent so much time in the studio, I didn't make new friends around Atlanta. You'd think I would've been partying all the time, given how strict my upbringing had been. But the opposite was true: I somehow felt that I didn't deserve to have fun—especially if my sisters couldn't be there to enjoy it with me. My life was directed by guilt.

I once met Jermaine Jackson in Atlanta. When I told him how I was feeling about going solo and leaving my sisters behind, he said, "Toni, it doesn't matter, because once you're famous you can bring them in." That was interesting advice since he was there working on "Word to the Badd"—a controversial song in which he criticizes his brother Michael. But Jermaine insisted that it wasn't vindictive. "I called Michael, and he was cool with me doing it," he said. I didn't respond—that was between him and Michael. But I was thankful that Jermaine tried to help me with my guilt. If any musical family could relate to what I was experiencing, it would be the Jacksons.

I eventually moved out of the extended-stay hotel into a two-bedroom, garden-style apartment in Dunwoody. On the weekends, I called home frequently—but I didn't share much about what was happening in the studio. I kept my updates very general: "Everything is going well," I'd tell Mommy. My mother ended our conversations by repeating her favorite line: "Don't forget about your sisters, Toni." My response was always silence.

CHAPTER 9

The Boomerang Soundtrack

Miracles do happen—and by the time I was twenty-four, I'd been blessed with three huge ones. For starters, Bill Pettaway spotted me at that Amoco station. A year later, I got signed by the hottest R&B production duo in the world. Then one day in the winter of 1991, a third miracle came along—and it was one I couldn't have dreamed up.

After weeks of negotiations, the execs at Paramount finally chose L.A. and Kenny to produce the *Boomerang* soundtrack. Everything at LaFace came to a halt. I'd been working with Tim and Ted, a team of producers that had been signed to the label. But once we got the soundtrack, L.A. asked me to drop everything so we could complete the demos for Anita Baker to hear.

We worked around the clock to get three songs done—and "Love Shoulda Brought You Home" was one of the tracks. When Kenny played the song for Anita, she didn't love it. "Can you let me hear another version?" she asked. So Kenny changed up the song: He left the chorus the same, but he rewrote the verses and changed the melody. "What do you think of it now?" he asked Anita. "I like it—but I don't know if it's going to work for me." Because of some personal circumstances, Anita couldn't contribute after all. "What are we going to do?" Kenny asked. "Who else could we get?" Anita's response that day turned out to be the third pivotal moment of my career: "Who's that girl on the demo? She can sing. Why don't you use her?"

Anita's suggestion that Kenny use me is what sparked the thought in him. A couple days later, L.A. called and told me the news: "You know that duet that Anita was going to do with Kenny?"

I paused. "Yes," I finally said.

"Well, you're doing the song with Kenny."

"Really!?" I shrieked.

"That's right," he said. "You're going to be on the soundtrack." I couldn't even speak.

Over the next few days, my "one song" on the soundtrack turned into four—Kenny reworked the entire album. "This is not the Toni Braxton project," the Paramount execs told him. So he scaled it back. Even still, I ended up singing "Love Shoulda Brought You Home" and "Give U My Heart." I also contributed vocals for a song called "Reversal of a Dog," with

LaFace Cartel. And it all happened very fast: We often stayed in the studio till three or four in the morning. L.A. and Kenny delivered the entire album within weeks.

My image had to be transformed quickly so I'd be ready to do press for the soundtrack. "We've gotta get you into artist development right now," said L.A. He and Kenny believed in spending money to make their artists look like stars—though it all came out of my project budget, of course. Pebbles was given the task of defining my look and updating my style. I got my eyebrows tweezed and shaped. A makeup artist picked out the right foundation, lipstick, and lashes for me (I had to get used to all that makeup . . . because I'd worn minimal makeup up until then, it felt a little heavy to me at first). Pebbles hired a clothing stylist, Bernard Jacobs, who chose the best styles for my shape. A shopper brought in clothing options for us to consider. I wanted to try big sweaters and fishnet stockings, and Pebbles told the shopper to go get them for me. She also picked out a colorful catsuit that she wanted me to wear—but I thought it was the most hideous thing I'd ever seen. I wanted to wear tight dresses that flared out at the bottom. "You're short and petite," Bernard told me, "so we really need to raise your hemlines." And for some reason, I became obsessed with a certain polka-dot dress that dropped off at the shoulder. "Please lose the polka-dot dress," Pebbles later told me. "It's just wrong"—and now that I look back on it, she was absolutely right.

Marie Davis, the hairstylist, sharpened my pixie cut. I'd been bleaching my sideburns—but she told me, "Let's make the sideburns work." She refined my cut and took me shorter, darkened my hair color, and made my sideburns really stand out. The whole process felt like being turned into Miss Congeniality! Pebbles even showed me how to pout my lips when I sang "Love Shoulda Brought You Home." She also taught me to love Chanel. "Chanel is your friend," said Pebbles. She had every kind of Chanel product you could imagine: purses, jeans, necklaces, the No. 5 perfume. She once bought me a Chanel sweatshirt, which I still have.

L.A. and Kenny brought in David Nathan, a voice coach and media trainer who taught me how to do interviews. Since my pitch is so deep, David brought in a speech pathologist who showed me how to speak in a higher voice. David then did mock interviews with me. Once my overhaul was complete, I loved the way I looked. Where were Pebbles and her team of magicians during my Homey Toni Braxton days? If only I'd known them then.

The *Boomerang* soundtrack debuted on June 30, 1992. I'll always remember the first time I saw the CD case. At the bottom of the front cover—beneath the names of renowned artists like Kenny, Shanice, Johnny Gill, and Boyz II Men—I saw three words: "Introducing Toni Braxton." If my career had ended right then and there, I would've felt like I'd made it.

L.A. and Kenny hoped the soundtrack would do well—but none of us could've anticipated that "Love Shoulda Brought You Home" would take off the way it did. That song reached number four on the charts. Another single, "Give U My Heart," my duet with Kenny, also became a hit, and the album sold millions of copies. My music was catching on across the country and around the world—but that didn't necessarily make me identifiable in person.

True story: Kenny and I once appeared on Arsenio Hall's show to sing "Give U My Heart," and afterward, I went out to the car to sit for a few minutes. When I returned for an after-party hosted by the show (my first party!), the security guard at the door wouldn't let me in. "I'm Toni Braxton!" I said insistently, but he didn't believe me. I had a cell phone on me—one of those giant flip phones that everyone had in the nineties—but it wasn't charged, so I couldn't call Kenny or anyone else to the door. People knew my voice—but they didn't always recognize my face.

Speaking of facial recognition, I got a nose job in 1992. I couldn't breathe very well when I first got to Atlanta, and Dr. Raj Kanodia told me that I should have sinus surgery. "You need to go ahead and fix that nose while you're at it," Pebbles told me. I'd been wanting to change my nose for years—I wanted it to be less broad. But because of the conservative ideas I was raised with, I struggled with the thought of altering my body. When Pebbles told me I needed a nose job, I somehow felt like I'd finally been given permission. When the surgeon examined my nose and noticed the fullness of my turbinates, he said, "I don't know how you're breathing." That gave me further permission to finally do what I'd been too scared to go ahead with on my own.

Strangely, I wasn't really nervous about telling my parents that I was planning to have a nose job—I think I was more fearful of the surgery itself than I was of their possible response. When I mentioned it to her on the phone, she just paused and said, "Oh Lord. Does that mean you have to go under anesthesia?" The answer was yes—and in the days leading up to the procedure, my parents started praying that I would make it through okay. My father didn't really say too much about my choice to have the nose job. He was just like, "Baby, just be careful out there in Hollywood." Mommy was totally supportive.

Three weeks after my initial consultation with Dr. Kanodia, I flew to Los Angeles to have the two-hour surgery done in his Beverly Hills office. That morning, my parents called me and said one last prayer for me on the phone. For some reason, I showed up in the doctor's office at 6:30 A.M. wearing jeans that were too big for me (they kept sliding down my butt!) along with a button-down white shirt and the brightest red lipstick I owned—I later had to take off that lipstick because your face must be bare before surgery. My pulse must've been through the roof, because I could practically feel my heart beating out of my chest. *Can I really go through with this?* I thought. Before I could back out, a nurse rounded the corner and offered me a cap to cover my head and a gown. Moments later, I was on a gurney, head covered, with the anesthesiologist standing over me. I clutched the side of the bed. "I want you to count backward, Toni," he said. I stared at him blankly for a moment, then began. "One hundred, ninety-nine, ninety-eight, ninety-seven . . ."—and then suddenly I was out.

When my eyelids slid open two hours later, I could hardly

breathe. After the surgery, the doctor had packed my nostrils with sponge and gauze—this was an old-school nose job. My throat was on fire from the breathing tubes the doctor had put down my throat. And my eyes felt painful and puffy. Later, when I gathered the strength to get up and look in the mirror, I just about scared myself. I looked like I'd been in a very big fight—one that I'd apparently lost. "Will the swelling go down?" I asked the doctor. "Yes, eventually," he told me. If there was any chance at all that he was wrong about that, my singing career would've suddenly been done. That's just how much of a hot mess my whole face was.

As it turns out, it took three years for the swelling to completely go away, and that was the point: L.A. and Kenny wanted the change to be gradual so it wouldn't look like I rushed out and had a nose job. And of course, I later got my boobies done—just about every female performer gets breast implants. Plus, I'd always been shaped like a gymnast—size double A breasts and thunder thighs. In fact, I wish I would've had lipo on my inner thighs. I've always hated them.

By the time I went in to see a Los Angeles surgeon about breast implants, I was more comfortable with the idea of altering my appearance, thanks to the nose job. But that didn't mean I was over my jitters about anesthesia or the postsurgery pain. In fact, I made an appointment for the procedure—but then I canceled it at the last minute because I got scared. During our pre-op appointment, the surgeon had talked me through all of the options for implants. "How full do you want your breasts?" he said. I didn't really know. "I think your frame would look good with a cup size that's somewhere be-tween a C and a D." I nodded. I then had to choose what kind of implants I wanted, silicone or saline—and I chose saline. "We'll make the incision in your underarm," he told me. He then explained the risks (most of which had to do with the an-esthesia) . . . which is right around the time I began wonder-ing again whether I was ready for this. In fact, that's probably why I ended up canceling our scheduled surgery.

But my courage returned—and a few weeks later, I put on that gown and surgical cap. This time when I awakened, I felt like I had an elephant sitting on top of my chest. That's just how intense the pressure was! They were swollen for a while, but in that case, it made them look even fuller. I loved how they looked. At last—Homey Toni Braxton had some curves. And finally, my taping days were done: Before I got the breast implants, my stylist would use duct tape beneath my tiny boobs to make it look like I had cleavage.

And can I be honest with you about something else? To this day, I am still happy I got that nose job. Yes, I wish I'd gotten it smaller, but the new nose did fit my face so much bet-ter. Making my bridge more narrow and my nostrils smaller gave my nose a more feminine look. And though my parents were scared for me to have the procedure, they liked the final result as much as I did. And a couple of my sisters were like, "tell me everything about the surgery—because I might have my nose done, too!"

Eight weeks after my nose job, we shot the video for "An-other Sad Love Song"—and yes, our plan worked, because no one seemed to notice a change. I also began performing live. After all those years of singing in church, the record company didn't have to do much to mold me as a live performer. And of course, once our first single debuted, I set out on a grueling promotional tour to every urban center around the country. I did radio lead-ins like "Hi, this is Toni Braxton!" I shook lots of hands, posed for countless photos, and sat for dozens of interviews. The hard work paid off: DJs really grasped on to my songs. "Who's the short girl with the chubby cheeks, the pixie haircut, and the big ol' butt?" people started asking. I never thought I had a big butt—though I do have Serena Williams thighs and an athletic build! But that wasn't important. What mattered is that I was getting a whole lot of attention for two songs that weren't even originally written for me. Thank you, Anita Baker.

AROUND THE TIME when *Boomerang* took off, my manager called me up one day. "L.A.'s brother likes you," he told me. "You don't have to be his girlfriend, but why don't you flirt with him a little? You're in the business now—you've gotta hang out with people sometimes." I'd worked with L.A.'s brother, Bryant, a few times—he was an A&R manager at LaFace, and he'd been overseeing the songs I did with Tim and Ted. I thought he was a nice guy, yet I wasn't interested in a romance. He was averagely attractive. But he just wasn't my type—a little too short.

On the day my manager called, my mind flashed back to

an experience I'd once had in Maryland. When I was nine-teen, I worked as a background singer for a rapper whose Cau-casian manager liked me—but the feeling wasn't mutual. He was older, overweight, and frumpy. "Girl," the rapper later told me, "if you want to be successful in this business, you're going to have to get with a few guys you don't like."

I thought my manager was right: A little flirting couldn't hurt, and it might even improve our business relationship. So I went out a few times with Bryant. On one of those dates, we started making out . . . and . . . one thing led to another. I've never been one to kiss and tell, so I'll just say that things went farther than I ever intended—and I regretted it to the twenti-eth power. I called my cousin Jackie and told her the details. "You'll get over it," she said. "He's a nice guy." But I wanted to end it.

That wasn't as easy as it sounds. Even when I went silent, which was my way of letting the whole thing fade away natu-rally, Bryant kept calling. And calling. And calling. Let's just say, I ended up continuing to see Bryant because I didn't feel like I could break it off without hurting my career given his connections. In retrospect, I should have followed my heart and walked away.

IN DECEMBER 1992, L.A. and Kenny began strategizing: How could they ride the wave of the soundtrack's popularity and quickly put out my first album? Back in those days, you couldn't just come out with an album suddenly—the record company had to slot you in, sometimes as far out as a year ahead of time. I lucked out with getting onto the *Boomerang* soundtrack because it was already in the works and had to be done so expediently. So L.A. and Kenny had to persuade Arista to get my project out by the following summer. Arista finally agreed.

The process of making that album happened superfast. Kenny had already written "Breathe Again," and he sang it for me as he played the instrumental on a cassette. I nearly cried the first time I heard it—the melody sounded just that beautiful to me. Some of the other songs, like "Seven Whole Days," were written right there in the studio. When you're creating a song, it's not necessarily a straightforward process: sometimes, you just play around with the lyrics and melody until you stumble upon something that feels right. "Try singing that line, Toni," Kenny would often say to me as we were working on a piece. Once I sang the melody, he would usually go back and rearrange some of the lyrics, then ask me to sing it again. We could go back and forth like that for hours.

A lot of people think that famous musicians live a rock-and-roll lifestyle—but when I was starting out, my life was anything but that. No one saw me around town partying: I was in the studio for twelve, fifteen, sometimes even twenty hours a day. I'd often leave the studio at six in the morning and be back there by noon. Even when I was at home, I'd sit and study music—that's what you do before you go back into the studio for the next session. At times, I would dig out some old Babyface or Anita Baker cassettes and study the music. I'd also listen to the songs Kenny and I actually worked on and think about how I would interpret them. For instance, when Kenny first gave me "Breathe Again," he was singing it on the demo—and I listened hard while thinking, How can I make this my own? And of course, I had to do a lot of fast memorizing of the melodies and lyrics because we had such a short time to complete the album. That's what many don't know: If you want to be a great musician, you first have to be a devoted student of music. That involves practicing strict discipline every single day. It's not all just about getting up on the stage to perform—most of the real work happens behind the scenes.

As hard as I was working on the album, I still made time to connect with my family. I talked with them by phone on most days once I was home from the studio. Mom had gone from angry about my choice to go solo to proud and fairly supportive (that is, as long as I remembered that I was supposed to circle back and get my sisters a deal). My parents drove down from Severn to Atlanta every couple of months just to spend time with me. I didn't really take them with me to the studio (our sessions were closed, so none of the artists brought others along). So they would hang at my apartment as I worked, and we'd often go out to eat in the evenings. My sisters stayed behind in Severn—and word once got back to my parents that they'd thrown a huge house party (with alcohol and everything!) while my parents were away . . . and I'm sure you can imagine how well my parents took that news.

From time to time, I'd fly all of my sisters to Atlanta and have them hang out with me. I wanted to give them a front-row seat in my new life as a solo artist, as well as to encourage them to keep their own musical dreams alive. "Keep practicing and working hard!" I'd tell them. While they were in town, we didn't do anything particularly glamorous: I'd just take them with me to Lenox or Phillips Mall so we could shop together. Sometimes, we'd stop in Claire's and buy a cheap pair of earrings.

On July 13, 1993—a short six months after the project had been green-lighted by Arista—my self-titled album hit the record stores. I was so excited when the first single, "Another Sad Love Song," made it to the top of the charts. Other hits followed: "Breathe Again," "You Mean the World to Me," "I Belong to You," and "How Many Ways." I can't tell you how appreciative I was that people were listening to my music—imagine me, a little country girl from Severn, suddenly having a hit record. What a gift. I wanted to include my sisters in my success and give them another shot at breaking in, so I featured all four of them in the video for "Seven Whole Days." Practically overnight, I became the newest R&B artist people were buzzing about. You want to know when I felt like I had "made it"? The day I received a Soul Train Music Award. For me, that honor was the ultimate one, since it came from the show that first inspired me to dream. And on top of all that, I even won my bet with L.A.: He actually bought me a baby-blue Porsche, which he had delivered.

My life changed dramatically. My private life was pretty ordinary, but whenever I went out in public, I suddenly felt like I was living the glamorous life. Gone were the days when

I could just roll out in my sweats, flip-flops, and no makeup. The paparazzi were usually close by, ready to snap a photo. People came up to me when I went to the grocery store—my short haircut was an instant giveaway. One time when I was stopped at an intersection, a couple guys pulled up and shouted, "Can we have your autograph?" Another time, I went out to dinner at a Houston's restaurant in Buckhead, Atlanta, and a group of girls followed me into the restroom. While I was in the stall, one of them said to me through the door, "I'm sorry to bother you, Miss Toni, but can we have your autograph?" I've always been so flattered when others show me appreciation—but it was a bit awkward to have that conversation while my stream of pee flowed down and hit the water in the toilet. And yes: Once I zipped up and washed my hands, I did give the girls my autograph. It's a privilege to have such amazing fans.

Whenever I would pop in at Neiman-Marcus in Lenox Mall, people would come up to me and say hello. Once when L.A. and I went there together, a woman stopped and said, "I love your haircut!" In moments like that, L.A. would often step aside and just observe the interaction: He was always gathering information on how to create the best image for his artists. After that lady commented on my hairstyle, L.A. said, "We'll have to make your sideburns even more of a strong detail." He was so good at finding ways to improve me and the many other entertainers on his record label.

My family was as thrilled as I was about the success of my first album. When I returned to my hometown to visit, Mom and Dad hosted a barbecue at their house. They surprised me by having a lot of extended family there. I knew my parents were proud and just wanted to celebrate me. But the truth is that I was fatigued. I'd been on the road for weeks, performing my butt off onstage and then offering hundreds of handshakes afterward. Hanging out with a whole group of family in Severn felt like work to me—and I had come home to get away from work. Don't get me wrong: I've always loved performing, and I'm so grateful for the millions who support my work. But no matter how passionate you are about what you do, there comes a moment when you need a break. I needed to catch my breath.

From obscurity to superstardom—that became my story in a matter of only months, and I was pinching myself during the whole ride. Back when I was a girl, I had repeatedly prayed for fame. Yet I'd forgotten to add the part about fortune. I'd become a celebrity, yes—but I was still waiting on the financial rewards. God is busy. That's why I've since learned I need to itemize.

CHAPTER 10

Grammy Nightmare

Right after I finished my first album, I got my sisters a record deal at LaFace—but they never released any music on the label. That's because the A&R manager who signed them—Bryant, L.A.'s brother—left for a job at Atlantic. Bryant asked Kenny if he could take my sisters with him. Kenny agreed.

In the interim, Trina and Traci got pregnant. Because Traci's pregnancy came after the Atlantic deal was signed, she wasn't allowed to stay in the group (record label execs will often call off a deal if a female artist becomes pregnant—no, it's not fair, but that's just the way it is). Towanda, Trina, and Tamar continued with their deal and later released the album *So Many Ways* as the Braxtons. It earned a couple golds abroad, but it didn't do so well here in the United States. I thought the album's producers tried to make my sisters sound like me, even though they were all younger. Even still, we were all hoping that the record would be a big hit, and I think my sisters were disappointed that it didn't blow up overnight the way mine did. I understand that disappointment, but here's the part that confounds me: I've often been blamed for it. Over the years, I've heard a certain complaint repeated from a couple of my sisters: "We helped you in your career—now why can't you help us?"

I've always acknowledged this: Performing as one of the Braxtons is what led to my deal with L.A. and Kenny. So when it came to helping my sisters get their own deals, I did a lot of legwork for them—and yet they've still said I'm not doing enough. I've finally come to a conclusion: As much as I love my family, I am only responsible for myself and my children. Period. But during my early days in the music business, I wasn't yet strong enough to stand in that truth.

With the success of my first album, L.A. and Kenny put a lot of thought into how they should market me for my second album and beyond. I felt like a bottle of ketchup—a product that had to be branded and sold. "She's so young," L.A. once said to Kenny, "and yet her voice is so mature." Sometimes they would have entire conversations about me as if I wasn't there. On one particular day in 1993, Daryl Simmons, a producer and a silent partner on a lot of my songs, had dropped by Atlanta's Doppler Studios to meet us.

"Maybe we should call her Toni Michele," said Kenny. "Or maybe she should just be Toni. That sounds young."

"But we don't want to make the mistake that people made with Johnny Gill," L.A. responded. "He was like a child with this big, giant voice. Maybe we should make her older so she can appeal to an older demographic."

Daryl finally piped up: "I like the name Toni Braxton. It's so distinct. Don't change her name." They paused, and I studied each of their faces.

"Well," L.A. finally said, "the name Toni Braxton will probably sell five hundred thousand more units. Let's stick with that." I didn't say a word. I think a lot of my success came from knowing when to shut the hell up.

L.A. and Kenny eventually concluded that I should be younger and sexier on the second album. I loved the music of other artists in my age group, like Mary J. Blige, and I wanted to sing the kind of dance hits that would involve stage choreography. Yet L.A. and Kenny wanted to put me at the piano on the stage, like Carole King. "She should just be a diva behind a mic," Clive protested. That's why they decided to save the whole piano thing for a future album—and I did eventually do one of those morning shows where they had me play and sing a song I wrote called "Best Friend." But even when I played, many people thought I was faking it. I wasn't. Though I signed on to LaFace as a singer-songwriter, I always had Kenny.

When it came to songwriting, I was no Kenny (at least not

yet!)—but he did encourage me. "You should get in the studio and write some songs," he'd tell me. "Maybe you could be part of a duo, like Jimmy Jam and Terry Lewis." He tried pairing me with this singer named Debra Killings, who played the bass and did a lot of background vocals for TLC. "You two could be like A Taste of Honey with 'Boogie Oogie Oogie,' " said Kenny. "You play the piano and Debra plays the bass." It was a good idea—but the energy never quite came together on that collaboration because I got caught up in other work.

Once a first album has been a hit, some artists feel an enormous pressure to produce a second album that's just as good or better. I didn't feel that way at all. In fact, my first record's success gave me a real surge of confidence. I couldn't wait to get into the studio. The creative process is hard work, yes, but it's also completely fulfilling when you finally come up with just the right lyrics or melody. That happened rather organically for the song called "You're Makin' Me High"—and as it turns out, *very* high.

First things first: I'd never taken a puff of anything. By now, I'm sure you've figured out that I was a late bloomer—so at twenty-six, I began working overtime to get out of the "church girl" box and really explore life. But one evening when someone gave me a blunt, I thought I'd try it. First of all, I was paranoid to even have it in my possession. "It's such a small amount that you won't go to jail for it," said the person who handed it to me. But I was still nervous—so I tucked it away in a shoebox in my bedroom. A couple nights later, I finally pulled it out, lit it, inhaled, and smoked the whole thing in one sitting.

I loved it—at least the first few times I smoked. I would watch the Chinese channel and think I actually understood what the actors were saying! But after smoking four or five Mary Janes over the following couple of months, I started to feel strange. Maybe marijuana relaxes some people, but it gave me a weird kind of déjà vu—I felt like I was reliving my entire life, scene by scene. It also made me giggle. A lot. Once that laughing was finished, I felt dizzy. And finally, my lightheadedness was followed by a horrible case of the munchies. Then one night while I was smoking, I had the most terrible panic attack I'd ever experienced. I decided it was time to stop— and I've never touched any drug since. When I admitted to Kenny that I'd experimented with marijuana, he just chuckled. "Who'd you try it with?" he said. I smiled but didn't answer. A couple weeks later in the studio, Kenny and I were working on a track by Bryce Wilson (Bryce gave the track to me, and I loved it so much that I let L.A. and Kenny hear it). That day, Kenny and I reworked the lyrics and came up with a song—"You're Makin' Me High." That's the one good thing that came out of my pot phase.

I CONTINUED TO hang out with Bryant from time to time. I'm sure he thought we were in a relationship, but I didn't see us as that serious. At one point, we would get together a couple times a month, but then I'd back away and we'd stop seeing each other for weeks at a time. I kept trying to tell him that it was over—but he wouldn't let it be over. I never wanted to see him again in private. But I did anyway—mostly because he was so involved with my sisters. The whole time my sisters were working with Bryant at Atlantic, I never told them about the nature of our relationship or how unhappy I was.

IN DECEMBER 1993, my manager called me with some news: The Recording Academy had asked me to be one of the artists to announce the nominees for the upcoming spring Grammy Awards ceremony. "When you're asked to announce," my manager told me, "it could mean that you'll be nominated." There was no guarantee of that, but it was still pretty exciting for me to show up at the venue at like five thirty in the morning, get my hair and makeup done, and then read off the nominees from a sheet that was handed to me. Hundreds of members of the press were gathered. When I looked down on the sheet and saw my name, I froze. My nominations were in three categories: Best Female R&B Vocal Performance (for "Another Sad Love Song"), Best New Artist, and Best Female Artist.

I was ecstatic—yet I didn't really have a chance to celebrate the moment. Bryant disapproved whenever I went out and did anything fun. He wanted to keep me to himself. Plus, my guilt resurfaced any time I accomplished something that didn't include my sisters, so in that way, Bryant was perfect for me. He endorsed my habit of staying home or with him all the time, and it was easier to blame him for that than to admit that I probably wouldn't have been out on the town anyway. When I look back on that time, I really hate it that I didn't go out and live it up. I had reached the biggest accomplishment in my career to date, and yet I didn't feel like I could celebrate.

My prep for the Grammys started weeks ahead of the ceremony. Right away, I knew one thing for sure: I wanted to wear a red dress. Why? Because I'd noticed that other artists had worn red when they'd received their first award. Maybe the color would bring me some luck. I chose a sheer, red, lace halter with small rhinestones on it. Very sexy.

In the days leading up to the ceremony, the jazz saxophonist Kenny G and I rehearsed "Breathe Again," the duet we would perform at the Grammys. During one of the rehearsals at the show's venue, Radio City Music Hall, I ran into Jody Watley. In 1987, she'd won a Grammy as Best New Artist. She'd been asked to return and present the Grammy to that year's winner. "I think you're totally going to win it!" she told me. She couldn't know that for sure, of course, but I still felt a surge of adrenaline. *Maybe I have a chance,* I thought. *This could be my big moment.*

On March 4, 1994, I attended the Grammys. I spent most of the day getting ready: hair (my signature short cut, just sharpened up a bit), makeup, and even red heels to go with the dress. I decided to keep my makeup super simple. "The dress should speak for itself," I told my stylist. By the time I stepped onto the red carpet, I felt like a princess.

So many of the stars I'd admired for years were actually

excited to meet me. "I love your music, Toni!" Billy Joel told me on the red carpet. I was stunned that he and other celebrities even knew my name! When I finally took my seat in my red halter dress, Bryant—my date that night—sat right next to me, but throughout the evening he barely spoke to me and didn't offer a single word of encouragement.

The moment finally arrived for the Best New Artist category. My parents—proud as ever—were there watching in the audience. As Jody Watley and Billy Joel read off the nominations, my heart raced every time a name was called. Belly. Blind Melon. Toni Braxton. Digable Planets. SWV. By the time Jody opened the envelope, I was sure SWV was going to win. "And the Grammy goes to . . . Toni Braxton!" The crowd erupted with applause. "Another Sad Love Song" played over the loudspeaker. I placed my palm over my forehead in disbelief as my eyes filled with tears. But those weren't tears of joy. What should've been one of the proudest moments of my life was ruined because I chose to share it with Bryant, who had been cold to me all night.

After my name was called, I hugged Bryant, handed him my purse, and made my way up to the stage. Once Jody handed me the gold-plated trophy, I opened a folded piece of paper and read a thank-you to just about everyone in the universe: God, my parents, my sisters, my brother and his family, L.A. and Kenny, Davett Singletary (VP of artist development at LaFace), Daryl Simmons, Bill Pettaway, Ernesto Phillips, the entire LaFace and Arista staffs, Clive Davis, my band,

Vernon Slaughter . . . and that's not even the full list. I even acknowledged the very man who made me feel nothing like a winner that night.

My career shifted into high gear after the Grammys (and by the way, my second win, the one for "Another Sad Love Song," happened off camera). Jon Avnet, the director for the Robert Redford film *Up Close and Personal*, asked me to do a song for the movie's soundtrack. Diane Warren, the award-winning songwriter, let Kenny and me hear a demo of a ballad she'd written—"Because You Loved Me." But since the soundtrack would be released in the same year that my record would be out (1996), L.A. thought it might be too much. "As an artist, you don't want to be overexposed," he said. In those days, the thinking was that fans might get tired of an artist who was all over the place—which is the total opposite of what's true today. "What do you think, Toni?" L.A. asked me.

I shrugged. "You're right. It's probably too much," I said, "and I don't really like the melody." The truth is that I was excited about doing the song, but I didn't think I had much of a right to my own opinion. That's why I usually just repeated whatever L.A. and Kenny said. So we passed on the project— and I acted like I was cool with that.

As the opportunities rolled in, my relationship with Bryant continued. Once when Bryant and I were visiting my parents in Maryland, I borrowed my mother's white Mercedes to drive my godson back to D.C. to drop him off. Bryant came with me, and on the way, we got into a big argument. I was so angry that I twisted the car's steering wheel and swerved onto the right curb of Pennsylvania Avenue. I will never forget that feeling. Never in my life had I wished that another human being would die.

I made a decision that day: I would never talk to Bryant again. The rage I felt in that moment lent me enough courage to end it. Over the next few weeks, Bryant called. A lot. But I didn't care anymore. Nothing he said or did could make me go back. For the first time in my adult life, I took a stand for myself. Nearly two decades after that incident, I'm still mastering how to do that.

CHAPTER 11

Bankrupt

M y first real payday came in 1996—the year my attorney added an amendment to my previous contract. Under this revised agreement, I was to receive an advance on future recordings. I thought I might get $30,000 more—but the total amount due to me after that adjustment was $1.6 million. The day I got the check, I sat and stared at it for a full six minutes. At last, I had some money.

Then again, $1.6 million isn't *really* $1.6 million. First, you've gotta pay taxes on that money. I did that right away. Then there are commissions—an artist's agents, lawyers, and managers each have to be compensated, and the payments can add up to 25 percent off the top. So after I handed over checks for all of those things, I had about $600,000 left.

Most people would call $600,000 a lot of money—and frankly, so did I. I purchased my first place, a four-bedroom house. I wanted a home large enough to accommodate my family when they came to visit—that's how a country suburban girl thinks. The home was just being built, so I added hardwood floors throughout, and I had two of the bedrooms combined into one long one. I then purchased a gorgeous mahogany Schimmel piano (which I still have in my living room to this day) and I leased a navy blue Cherokee.

There were perks to being famous—and finally having a little money to go along with that fame. I went from staying in basic hotel rooms to sleeping in the double suite penthouse at the Four Seasons in New York. The first time I saw the space, I was blown away: The walls were covered with gorgeous art, the sheets were super luxurious, and I felt like I'd just stepped into a scene from *The Great Gatsby*. Totally spectacular. My only regret was having no one to share the room with me. At the time, I didn't have a boyfriend—and though my family sometimes visited me, they weren't with me during that first stay at the hotel.

Speaking of my family, our connection had grown tighter as my career ascended. Mom might've originally disapproved of my choice to go solo, but once I was solidly on that path, she got behind me 100 percent. She and my dad called me often and came to see me whenever they could. When I'd travel home to Severn, they proudly invited their friends to come to the house. And any chance I got, I flew my sisters in to spend time with me either when I was on the road or in Atlanta. I wanted to give them a front-row seat to my singing career—and to keep alive their own dreams of making it big.

As for the fabulous vacations that usually come with fame, I didn't really take any—but that doesn't mean I didn't get out of the country at times to perform. I crisscrossed Europe and visited places I'd only read about—Berlin, Paris, Brussels, London, Rome, Milan. Arista's parent company, BMG, is headquartered in Germany, so I passed through there a lot. The crazy part is that when you're working overseas and darting from one city to the next, there really isn't much time for leisurely sightseeing. But at the very least, a chauffeur might point out a city's most famous sites (as in the Eiffel Tower and Big Ben) during the drive to or from the airport.

I once traveled to Tokyo for work—and I came home with a funny story. I adored Japan itself, but I wasn't in love with the fact that so many things on the room service menu were raw (lots of sushi!). So I decided to order the Kobe steak—and I loved it, so I kept ordering it for a few nights. How was I supposed to know that Kobe steak is one of the most expensive cuts of meat in Japan? At the end of the week, my room service bill was more than $4,000! I didn't have enough money with me to cover the bill, so the record company settled the bill—and I paid them back a couple months later.

Fame comes with another big change—your community expands to include other celebrities. L.A., who was always trying to get me to step out on the town with a hot celebrity man of the moment, thought that would do wonders for my image. At one point, he was pressing me to show up to an awards ceremony with Wesley Snipes—but I was too embarrassed to even ask Wesley because of a situation that had previously cropped up. Out of nowhere, Wesley apparently sent flowers to me at my record company. The only problem is that my publicist never actually told me that he'd sent the flowers—I swear that I had no idea. That kind of thing happens all the time in my business—your team handles a lot of your day-to-day details, and word doesn't always reach you about all that has been written about you, said to you—or, in my case, sent to you. Half the time, you read something in the paper about yourself, and you're going, "What is that all about? I didn't even know that happened." So anyway, I was out on the road doing a show when Wesley's delivery arrived, so my publicist probably just hadn't gotten around to mentioning the gift. And by the way, I had no clue about the intention behind the nice gesture: I'll never know whether Wesley was interested in me, or if he was simply a fan of my music. But either way, someone in my camp had put the word out in the press that Wesley had sent me those flowers. So once I actually heard (weeks later!) about the gift, I called Wesley myself—and he seemed a bit annoyed. He goes, "How do I know that your publicist isn't on this phone right now, writing down everything I'm saying?" I apologized profusely that the news had been leaked—maybe he had a girlfriend at the time, and he didn't want her and the rest of the world to know that he'd sent me flowers. Fair enough—but my point is that this was exactly the kind of "What the hell?" experience I suddenly began dealing with in my new world. Crazy, right?

I never had a fling with Wesley—but I did once have a short romance with Shemar Moore, the model and actor. He and I met when he appeared in my video for the song "How Many Ways," which was on my first album. We shot the video on location in Miami. And he had just gotten his role on *The Young and the Restless*. It was never anything serious between us—to this day, we're cool as friends. If he walked in the room right now, he'd be like, "Hey, T—what's up?" Yet from the day I saw him on the set, I have to admit that I did think he was cute. "My agent called and asked me, 'Do you want to be in a Janet Jackson video or a Toni Braxton video?' " he said jokingly when we met. "I go, 'Janet Jackson.' But then I heard that Janet had already picked another guy—so that's how I ended up with you." We both snickered—me less so than him. *What a prick,* I thought. In the following few months, we'd call each other and get together when we were in the same city.

In between hanging out with Shemar, straightening out drama with Wesley, and jetting around the world for performances, I did my share of shopping. And in fact, I rarely had to plunk down my own credit card: The celebrity life comes with clothes galore. From Gucci to Manolo Blahniks and beyond, I received so many (free!) dresses, shoes, and handbags, and for a fashionista like me, few upsides of the famous life could compare. My stylist could call up a designer and get a dress for me right off the runway! "I need that for Toni Braxton," he'd say—and many times, I would get exactly what I wanted. If I requested a dress to wear for an awards show or an event, I usually had to return it. But that didn't matter too much—because there were always more cute items coming in for the next appearance. PS: I could wear just about anything worn by Kate Moss because we both have a short torso and long legs . . . the only thing I'd have to change about one of her dresses was the hemline. Once when I performed for Princess Diana, I wore this blue Calvin Klein dress that Kate had just worn on the runway. Loved it!

Using the money from that big check, I decided it was time to do what most celebrities get done when they first get a few dollars: I spruced up my home. "You've gotta get your house decorated," L.A. had told me. "You don't want it to look like you went down to the store and picked out a living room set." So I hired an incredible decorator, Tom Pharr. In the end, the entire house was so charming . . . very French. Tom even got it onto the cover of *Southern Living* magazine. After getting settled into my new home, I also helped my family financially—I bought cars for my mother and sisters. Once I'd made those purchases, I still had $300,000 in my account. I figured that was plenty for me to live on—mostly because I didn't know what awaited me just around the corner.

MY SECOND ALBUM, *Secrets,* hit during the summer of 1996. The self-titled debut record had catapulted me center stage in the R&B world—but it was album number two that actually turned me into a crossover success. For my sophomore effort, the legendary hit maker Diane Warren offered me another song that I wasn't feeling—I thought it sounded a bit too Disney. She also offered it to Céline Dion, who turned it down. But L.A. and Clive thought it was perfect for me. "Trust me," L.A. said, "you should take it. I promise you it'll be one of the biggest songs of your career." That's how I ended up with a little song you might've heard of called "Un-Break My Heart," which spent fourteen weeks at number one on the adult contemporary chart. I guess Céline and I each ended up with the song we were supposed to have.

I'd always wanted to let out my inner sexpot—and on *Secrets,* I got my chance. In the video for "You're Makin' Me High," I swiveled my hips while wearing a white, formfitting catsuit (Pebbles finally got her wish!). The higher the split, the better I liked the dress. The deeper the neckline, the more eager I was to show off some cleavage. Bille Woodruff, the video director for all the songs on my second album, encouraged me to be sexy. Not only did I want to finally put behind me all those years I spent as a Plain Jane preacher's kid, I yearned to feel like the sensuous, desirous woman I was evolving into.

L.A. encouraged that. "You should keep that sexy thing going," he told me. "It works." He's the one who suggested that I pose for that provocative *Vibe* cover—the one that appeared on newsstands in June 1997. "You need to do something risky," he said. And risky it was: I appeared to be nearly nude on that cover. Since I had my new toys by then (I'd had my boobies done!), I was okay with exposing my body—and I wanted to feel sexy so badly. Plus, I loved and trusted the photographer, Daniela Federici—I'd worked with her before, and she always knew how to make me look tall and lean. The truth is that I was actually wearing underwear—but my panties were Photoshopped out. The first time I saw the cover, even I was a little remorseful—that was a lot of skin to show. But the move was all part of the label's plan to create an image of me as a sex symbol. Part of singing is acting—and part of acting is creating a fantasy.

The worldwide success of "You're Makin' Me High" and "Un-Break My Heart" made Clive certain about one thing: I could have the same crossover appeal as Whitney Houston. So Clive, Kenny, and L.A. decided to send me out on tour with Kenny G, whose "Songbird" single had made him one of the country's hottest adult contemporary artists. I'd already proven that I could perform live: After my first album, I'd attempted to wow crowds during a series of tour dates I did with Frankie Beverly and Maze; my sisters were my background singers at the time. "You've already crossed over," L.A. told me. "Now we need to take it a step higher." So I agreed to tour with Kenny G and open for him. Sixty percent of the profits would go to him (it was his tour . . .) and the remaining 40 would come to me. A month after I made the choice to do the tour, I got a call from L.A.

"The black tour promoters are planning to boycott your tour," he said. Tour promoters organize, publicize, and oversee live concert events on behalf of artists. Among other tasks, they book the venue, set the price for the event to ensure that it is profitable, and orchestrate all on-site labor. Tour promoters—also known as concert promoters—negotiate a contract with the artist (usually through the artist's agent) whose tours they are managing. Unfortunately, like many other industries in America, there's some segregation among tour promoters—for instance, black tour promoters tend to have relationships with black artists, and white tour promoters tend to get access to white artists.

"Kenny G already has his own white promoters," L.A. explained. "So the black promoters are locked out of your concert tour. That's why they're angry with you."

I had no idea how to handle the situation—which is why I began backpedaling. "Maybe I shouldn't do the tour," I told L.A. After all, I hadn't yet signed a contract.

But Clive squashed my idea. "You have to do the tour," he said. "This is how Whitney made the crossover. You're too black to be white and too white to be black. That's why it's so important that you straddle the fence."

Around that time, I performed at the Soul Train Music Awards, held at the Shrine Auditorium in Los Angeles. Just as I was about to go out onstage, one of my managers pulled me aside.

"If anyone comes up to you and asks, 'Are you Toni Braxton?' do not answer," she said.

I wrinkled my forehead. "Huh? What's going on?"

"Just keep walking if anyone calls out your name," she told me.

With my nerves a little rattled by her comment, I walked out and sang for the audience, then made my way back to the greenroom. On my way out of the building, I didn't even stop to sign autographs or shake hands, fearing someone might be after me. In the limo, my tour manager finally explained herself. "Kenny G's people are trying to serve you papers," she said. The concert's floor manager had passed that news along to my manager just before she'd cautioned me. "They're going to sue you if you don't do the tour." I couldn't be served if I didn't confirm my identity—and that's why my manager had asked me to shun anyone who came up to me.

I was as astonished as I was mortified. Though I'd mentioned that I was reconsidering whether I'd do the tour because of the issues with the black promoters, I hadn't actually bowed out. In fact, tickets were already being sold.

So I decided that I'd better do two things: accompany Kenny G on that tour, and work out some kind of deal with the disgruntled promoters. As for the latter, I called up a record producer who had relationships with a lot of the promoters, and asked him to negotiate a deal. He did—which is how some of the black promoters ended up on my tour.

Kenny G and I never talked about what happened—for all I know, he didn't even realize his manager had tried to serve me with a suit. That's the way things often go in the music biz. On November 6, 1996, I set out on a tour with Kenny to perform in forty-two cities across the United States; once the U.S. tour was over, I'd go on to Europe for a series of concerts alone.

But everything wasn't settled. Kenny G's people were still nervous about whether I'd follow through with the tour, so they set up an arrangement to hold half of my earnings in escrow. This meant that I only received 20 percent of my 40 percent of the profits until the end of the show. My record company's execs didn't want to loan me any money for the tour, mostly because they had a personal beef with one of my managers. So in order to cover the costs associated with all of those concerts—the band, the sets, the props, the lights, the hair and makeup, the wardrobe, the background singers and dancers, the tour buses, the fuel, a couple of drivers, and a full crew to transport that whole operation from one city to the next—I took out a business loan from Arista for a million dollars. That had to be repaid at a rate of between $25,000 and $35,000 a week while I was still on the road. Those payments came from ticket sale earnings, and I put anything extra back into the show. Bottom line: Every week, I was barely breaking even—but even still, I forged ahead and did the best that I could to manage everything.

ONE EVENING DURING a break from the tour, I sat and surfed through the hotel's TV channels. I happened to stop on ESPN, which I never watch—but a handsome man on the screen caught my eye. "He's really cute," I said to my security guy. "I know him," he responded. "That's Curtis Martin—he plays for the New England Patriots." My eyes were still glued to the screen. "Do you want to meet him?" he asked. "You know him like *that*?" "Well, a friend of mine knows him like that," he explained. I smiled, nodded, and didn't think too much more about it—until the day, a few weeks later, when my security guy told me he'd arranged to have Curtis come to see me perform on the weekend when the tour stopped in Boston.

After the show, at around 10 P.M., Curtis and I met in the living room area of my hotel suite—I hadn't had time to see him backstage, so my team arranged for us to sit down together back at the hotel (I felt perfectly safe because my security guy, who'd assured me that Curtis was a gentleman, would be standing by right across the hall). Before Curtis arrived, I changed out of my stage dress and into an oversized log-cabin-style plaid sweatshirt and some jeans. My face was still done up. "Wow," he joked when I greeted him, "I thought you were going to answer the door wearing a sequined gown." "Why would I do that?" I said, laughing a little. "I had to get comfortable." I welcomed him in and we sat across from each other on the couch.

I immediately felt at ease with Curtis—talking with him seemed effortless. We covered a whole range of subjects: religion (he had just become a Christian and was very excited about his new faith), sports (his passion for football), and music. We ordered room service, and between bites of my burger and fries and his steak, our hour of conversation somehow turned into several. By 4 A.M., I already knew I liked him—a lot.

That conversation quickly progressed into a relationship. We began calling and texting each other many times a day. We'd sometimes talk so late into the evening that one of us would fall asleep on the phone. He came to more of my performances—like when he traveled to meet me in Pittsburgh (his hometown) when the tour stopped there. I even carved out time to go to one of his games. Our romance was a whirlwind—and I enjoyed every moment of the ride. I still call Curtis my first real love. And though I eventually discovered that he is six years younger than me (he once couldn't rent a car because he wasn't yet twenty-five!), our age difference didn't matter at all. What did matter was the instantaneous connection and real friendship that we built with one another.

We spent a lot of our time talking about religion—he had the kind of zeal that comes with being a baby Christian. "I love the way you were raised," he'd say when I'd tell him about all the time we spent in church. He also loved the fact that I was so green—I'd been exposed to so little about the world and pop culture during my childhood, which is why I often found myself pretending that I knew things that I had absolutely no clue about. "Stop pretending," Curtis would tell me. "It's okay to be green." Before he got into pro football, Curtis had an upbringing that I would call very street—and the discipline that came with playing football went along with the discipline he was developing in his newfound Christianity.

One evening a few weeks into our relationship, Curtis brought up the topic of sex. "How do you feel about waiting?" We'd been kissing and hugging a lot up to that point, but I'd decided that I didn't want to rush intimacy—and I told him that. "For me, sex is for when you get married," he said. "I can't wait to make love to my wife one day." Because of his religious beliefs, he'd chosen to become celibate. I agreed. *This man must really like me if he's telling me this*, I thought. I actually already knew he liked me—but his statement about wanting to wait for marriage made me feel like he respected me. I also admired him for standing by his convictions—something not that many people do anymore. So that night, we agreed that we'd wait—and we did. I knew what the Bible said about sex, so deep down, I realized we should refrain. And besides that, I figured it was worth waiting to have intimacy if our love story would one day end with a happily ever after.

I loved how fervent Curtis was about his faith—but I have to confess that, at times, it was a little off-putting. He was coming fresh to Christianity after a childhood with no religious faith—whereas my childhood experience with Christianity was one filled with fear and condemnation. "You have to unlearn some of the things you were taught," Curtis would tell me. He was at the juncture where you think you know everything—and the tendency is to Bible thump and quote a lot of Scripture. But because I knew he was such a young Christian—and because I appreciated the intensity that he had about his faith—I often just set aside my slight annoyance.

In-between all those long conversations (and when I could break away from my tour for a day), Curtis and I actually had a lot of fun together. He once took me to see The Blue Man Group in Boston. He also took me out to a lot of nice restaurants. When others would spot us together, I did my best to steer the limelight toward him—back then, he wasn't as much of a star football player as he has become in the years since, and I didn't want my career as a singer to overshadow his accomplishments. In our quiet moments away from the public, Curtis was quite romantic: He wrote me poems and read me passages from Song of Solomon in the Bible. By the time I wrapped up the U.S. part of my tour and prepared to fly off to Europe, I knew one thing for certain: I wanted to spend the rest of my life with Curtis.

WHILE I WAS on tour in Europe, it quickly became apparent that I couldn't keep up with all the payments I owed Arista. Even once I counted the money I had in escrow, I was still falling into a financial hole. The tour was just too costly. "We've gotta cut back on the scenery for the sets," one of my managers told me. He didn't show me any numbers, but I could tell by the look on his face that we were in trouble. "This whole tour is costing too much," he said. So I scaled it all back by several thousand per show.

I also did everything I could to cut my personal costs. I sold my home in Atlanta and instead bought a condo in Los Angeles—since we were doing most of our studio recording in L.A. by that time, purchasing a place there meant drastically reducing hotel and travel expenses. And I invested a lot of my own money into keeping the show going. When my sisters joined me as backup singers on the European leg of the tour, I paid them out of my own pocket—so I could reduce the deficit for the tour. I also paid for Mint Condition (my favorite band!) to perform with me during the tour. With all those expenses, my checking account funds began dwindling from a strong six figures to a weak five.

As if my stress level wasn't already off the charts, another problem cropped up during this time. I began to suspect that my father was having an affair. He'd often ask me to get free tickets for some of the people at his job at Baltimore Gas and Electric Company (he'd left E. J. Korvette once it closed down back in 1980). I happily arranged tickets for his colleagues. One time, he got tickets for his coworker to attend a concert. Mommy went to the concert as well, but her seat was all the way on the other side of the arena. After the show, a woman who was one of my assistants at the time told me, "Toni, your father's got a girlfriend! I saw him kissing on some lady"—but I wasn't quite sure whether to believe her. Another time when my sisters were on a tour with Luther Vandross, Daddy flew out to meet them in Vegas. He brought one of his coworkers with him—you guessed it, this same woman—and her mother. They all stayed in a large suite. And in Severn, this woman would often call my parents' house and say, "Is Reverend Braxton there?" Sometimes, my father would suddenly have to go after one of those calls. Once when I was home visiting, Daddy even went out in the middle of a snowstorm after this woman rang; he claimed he had to "work" and that he needed to stay overnight. To this day, Mommy says that she never saw the signs—but they were abundantly clear to me.

I MET KEYBOARDIST Keri Lewis on the Kenny G tour. Keri was a member of Mint Condition, the band I'd hired to open for me. After our show, I'd often hang out with the whole band—when you're on the road with people for weeks and months, a bond naturally develops. *These guys are a lot cuter in person than people even know,* I thought. I especially thought Keri was handsome—and helpful. One afternoon as we prepared for a show, my programmer somehow messed up some of the drumbeats. "I'll reprogram it for you," Keri told me. "Don't worry about it."

Keri grew up in Minnesota. So when our tour arrived in Minneapolis, he and Stokley Williams (Mint Condition's lead singer) showed me around their hometown. Later, when the tour stopped close to Maryland, we drove down to visit my family. "Keri likes you!" my cousin Jackie told me once she'd met him. "No, he doesn't!" I said insistently. "It's not even like that. We're just friends." After all, I was still with Curtis. But when Keri eventually mentioned he had a girlfriend in Minnesota, I have to admit that I was a little annoyed—and I even surprised myself with that reaction because I was still very much in love with and committed to Curtis. One weekend when I offered to hang out with Keri, he said he wanted to spend time with his girlfriend instead. "Why are you so upset?" my cousin said when I told her about it later. "I think it's because you like him!" she declared. I denied that, of course—but at that point, I did admit to myself that our friendship seemed to be getting tighter and tighter. Even still, I put my connection with Keri at the back of my head—because front and center was my romance with Curtis.

DURING THE WEEK the tour stopped in Brussels, Bert Padell, then my business manager, called me from New York with some bad news. "Muscles, you're running out of money." Bert always called me "Muscles" because he said I seemed pretty fearless for a new artist. "We're already in the red. We've got less than fifty thousand dollars left."

"What do you mean?" I said. "Don't I have a royalty check coming?"

"You do," he explained. " 'Un-Break My Heart' is selling a bazillion copies, so that money is coming. But until then, you still need to take a personal loan to cover some of the show's expenses."

I did that—and I prayed that the coming royalty check would be enough to bail me out. After that big contract rene-gotiation, the $1.6 million of additional royalties I'd received had put me in the black. But when the following royalty state-ment showed up, I saw a figure that still shocks me—it was less than $2,000. That's because once the record company had recouped their money for the expenses related to my album and tour, less than two grand is what was left for me. "We'll ask the record company to loan you more money," my man-ager told me. But the Arista execs wouldn't budge. Since they didn't seem to want to work out a deal, I called L.A. directly. He didn't return my calls—and I had no idea what the record company might've been telling him about my situation, since we'd both had so many people speaking on our behalf.

That's when I began reckoning with a devastating reality: I might never get out of my predicament. The accolades may have been rolling in—I'd won five Grammys, five American Music Awards, and three MTV Video Music Awards by the end of 1997—yet I came back from Europe with little to show for my stardom. My debts totaled nearly $4 million.

In December 1997, I sued LaFace and Arista. I loved L.A. and Kenny like brothers, and I will always consider them my original music family—but in business, you sometimes have to make hard choices. The only way I could get the money I deserved was to sue. Even under the renegotiated agreement, I was receiving a much lower percentage of royalties than a bestselling artist typically earns. My records had sold an estimated $200 million worldwide—yet I was getting an average of just thirty-five cents per album.

One of my managers was hopeful that we could work out a deal with the label that would return me to solvency. "For an artist of your caliber, bankruptcy would be suicide," he said. "If you file, it will be the beginning of your demise. The industry will never forget it." But I had other voices in my ear that were just as persuasive. Barry Hankerson, whom I'd hired as a manager, told me, "You're too deep in the hole to make this work." He explained that the RIAA, a trade organization that represents recording industry distributors, was trying to change a law so that if any artist declared bankruptcy, any contract that an artist had signed with any person or company could become null and void—except for the artist's recording contract. "You need to hire some lawyers and fight," he said. So on January 23, 1998, I did what I thought I had to do to save my financial life: I filed for Chapter 7 bankruptcy.

CHAPTER 12

Headlines and Heartache

Ascarlet "B"—that's what I felt like I had stamped on my forehead during the entire bankruptcy process. I cried a lot. And daily. I just couldn't believe I'd allowed myself to get into this situation. When I called my mother and told her what I was feeling, she tried to comfort me. "You can always come home," she said. "It's all in God's hands." She and Dad flew to Los Angeles to visit me right away. My father, trying to support me, offered to sell the Rolex watch I'd given him as a Christmas gift. I might have my issues with my family, but one thing will always be true: We come together during a crisis.

Inspectors showed up nearly a dozen different times at my two-bedroom condo in Century City to audit my personal property—everything from my furniture and my artwork to my designer dresses and my awards. I wasn't home, so my assistant answered the door. "Where are the Grammys?" the assessor asked my assistant immediately when he arrived. In fact, the assessors only seemed interested in the Grammys—which is why I felt like they were purposely trying to humiliate me.

On another occasion, an assessor came to take stock of some belongings I'd put in a storage facility. I chose not to be there that day—too painful. So my assistant called to give me an update. "They've got all your stuff out," he said, "and it's starting to rain." My belongings were eventually put back in the unit, but not before a couple things were water damaged. In the end, I handed over many of my most valuable possessions—including all five of my Grammys.

Completely mortified—that's how I felt during the entire process of the bankruptcy. It was like being Cinderella when the clock strikes midnight and you have to give back the glass slipper. When you declare bankruptcy, all of your credit is frozen—which means that none of my credit cards worked. And all of my bank accounts were seized. Thankfully, I did get to live in my condo while they were assessing it. A couple days after I filed, Curtis gave me $10,000 in cash to live on. "Don't worry about everything," he said. "You're going to be okay." But even though I was trying to act strong, I felt broken. All I could do was cry and consume sugar: I ate Twizzlers and Kit Kats like crazy. My emotional low point came one evening when I'd returned to my condo after the inspectors had been there. I pulled into the garage and just sat there in my truck:

I couldn't quite bring myself to go upstairs after knowing the inspectors had been in my house, touching all my personal items. I felt naked. Invaded. Exposed. Finally, after a few minutes of cupping my hands in my face over the steering wheel, I opened the truck door and dragged myself through the front door. I went into the kitchen. Everything seemed in place. I then walked over to a mirror in the living room and just stood there and stared at myself. I felt so ugly and ashamed. As I peered, the tears began to topple down my shirt. I made my way into the bedroom, pulled the curtains together to make the room completely dark, and I just lay there and wept. I couldn't believe what a mess my life had become—and how it all seemed to happen so quickly.

As word of my filing reached the press, hurtful headlines like TONI BRAXTON: UN-BREAK MY WALLET and BRAX DONE abounded. The most bewildering part of the ordeal was the impression those news stories gave to the public: Over and over again, I was accused of squandering my earnings on an extremely lavish lifestyle. That was simply a lie. And hearing it was like standing naked in front of the world, with no way to cover myself. I felt completely humiliated—and I wanted to at least give my side of the story. That's why I chose to appear on *The Oprah Winfrey Show.*

On February 27, 1998, I flew to Amarillo to tape an episode of the show—Oprah and her crew had temporarily relocated to Texas because she was in the middle of that big Texas beef trial. I admired Oprah—I was one of her biggest fans at the time. Even before she had her national show, I used to tune in to *People Are Talking,* her Baltimore show. She always seemed to be helping people, and I believed she would somehow help me. I thought that going on her show would finally give me the opportunity to set the record straight about my bankruptcy.

On the day of the taping, Oprah came to my backstage room to briefly greet me. "Hello, Toni!" she said. "See you out there!" I was so excited to meet her (and a little mad that my hair wasn't right that day!).

As a setup to our interview, a prerecorded piece was played for the audience. "Five years after the thirty-one-year-old pop sensation made it big, she has filed now for bankruptcy," Oprah narrated in part of the segment's voice-over. "At her elegant Los Angeles condominium, appraisers are now taking stock of her possessions. Her baby grand piano. Her Gucci silverware. Her Porsche and Lexus. They're even counting her shoes . . . and her Grammys." Right after that segment finished, Oprah continued the introduction. "Toni Braxton has sold over one hundred seventy million dollars' worth of records, yet she says she's going to be out of a home— homeless—in sixty days. In her first television interview since filing for bankruptcy, she's here to share her story with us. Please welcome five-time Grammy winner . . . Toni Braxton!" I walked out smiling. The audience cheered, and then Oprah and I hugged. I took my seat.

"Nobody can believe that you're gonna be broke," Oprah said. "Is that true?"

"Yes, it's true," I said.

"And how did that happen—why did you have to file?"

"Well, I had to file because, first of all, like you said, I was broke," I said, shifting in my chair. "I had no money and I was very surprised. But let me also start by saying it wasn't always like that. I came to my record company, and I was so happy to be there working with fabulous producers. They introduced me to everyone, and I believed and had faith in everyone, and because I allowed all my finances to become everyone else's finances, that's pretty much how I got here."

"And that *is* the key," said Oprah. "Do you take responsibility for the situation you're in right now?"

I nodded. "One hundred percent," I said. "It's my fault because I trusted and I believed," I explained. A couple minutes after that exchange, things started to go south.

"When you've got Gucci silverware and baby grand pianos, and you're used to wearing five-, and six-, and seven-thousand-dollar gowns, and spending five hundred dollars on a pair of shoes, it's a long drop," Oprah said. "So how does that make you feel?"

"My image is much bigger than the dollars," I said. "The expensive dresses and shoes—I was financing personally the image that everyone sees."

"But most people are—because the old studio days are long gone with Elizabeth Taylor," said Oprah.

"Yes, but if someone is making one hundred seventy or one hundred eighty million dollars," I said, "and I got one-twentieth of a hundredth of that, it makes it almost virtually impossible." My throat tightened.

"I read that you were upset about stories that your overspending caused this," Oprah said later in the interview. "Because it would appear—and you can explain to us whatever you want to explain to us—but it would appear that, even if you don't believe that you got the percentage you felt you should've got, you still knew that there was a certain amount of money coming in. And you overspent that amount of money."

"Well I was doing math," I said. "One plus one is two all day long, all across the world. And I was still coming up negative. So I'm thinking that I've sold over twenty million records, so money's gonna come in . . . but there was no money coming in."

"That's the key there, Toni—are you spending money when there's no money coming in?"

"I was spending money on touring," I explained. "Touring is very expensive. I invested a lot of money in my career."

After the interview, I was deflated. Given my perceived celebrity lifestyle, it was easy for the public to jump to conclusions about my money troubles. But I didn't earn "millions"— Arista did. Yes, the record company sold nearly two hundred million dollars' worth of albums, but I received a mere fraction of that money. And the vast majority of my expenses were marketing costs that should've been underwritten by my label. That would later be proven in court.

The episode aired on Monday, March 2, 1998—and it immediately changed my career. People were already talking about my bankruptcy, of course, but the new headlines became ARTIST SPENDS MILLIONS ON GUCCI FLATWARE. I made my mistakes—and as I told Oprah, I take full responsibility for those blunders. But I was still hurt by how I was painted in the media.

Dozens of entertainers have declared bankruptcy. TLC filed. So did Kim Basinger, Larry King, Cyndi Lauper, Burt Reynolds, Willie Nelson, and Cathy Lee Crosby, just to name a few. And a lot of people seem to forget the long list of businessmen and leaders who've gone broke—including Walt Disney, Donald Trump, and presidents Ulysses S. Grant, Abraham Lincoln, and Thomas Jefferson. I'm not saying that this absolves me or anyone else of personal accountability. But here's what I am saying: An extravagant lifestyle is not *always* what leads to bankruptcy—and it is not what led to mine. Clive Davis even wrote in his 2013 memoir that I went bankrupt because of my tour costs.

Yes, I bought nice items for myself—I once said in a TV interview that I'd spent some of my earnings on things like high thread count sheets and Fabergé glasses as I was decorating my home. This is the part of that story that didn't get aired: I purchased a lot of my home accessories at discount stores such as TJ Maxx. And you have to remember that even when I was making purchases at places like Tiffany & Co. (usually to get a gift for someone in the industry), I actually had hundreds of thousands of dollars in the bank. I'm not going to apologize for treating myself with nice purchases when I actually had the money for them: I was living well within my means. Then much later—and rather suddenly—I realized my financial picture had changed dramatically because of the way Arista structured my contract and charged me for tour costs. At that point, I started using my own money to stay afloat professionally—and I wasn't spending any extra money on myself.

Here is the straightforward truth about what happened: I signed a bad contract. I then trusted other people to do what I should've done for myself—pay attention to every cent. In short, I gave away my power—and I've often been furious with myself for doing that. I allowed others' opinions to matter more than my own, and I've paid a big price for doing so. In the years since, I've gone through the same process of forgiving myself that any human being would have to go through. And along the way, I've learned that debt isn't a symptom of some kind of moral bankruptcy—it's simply a sign that I should've managed my tour costs better. And while going broke doesn't make me broken, I've still had to confront a hard reality: I took my eye off the ball. Period. And bankruptcy was the tool I used to start over.

Years after that show, I thought about writing a letter to Oprah. I actually sat and typed one out. I heard that Iyanla Vanzant, the life coach, had written a note to Oprah, and they actually repaired their relationship. That gave me the idea that maybe I could also clear the air with Oprah. But then again, their situation was different: Oprah and Iyanla were friends, and I was just a guest Oprah once interviewed. I can understand that she was only doing her job and asking the questions that everyone else was thinking. That's why I sat my hurt aside and did my best to make peace with it. I never sent my letter.

As the world focused on my bankruptcy, I tried to move on from my mistake—but it's hard to do that when you're feeling ostracized. The phone stopped ringing. People in my industry didn't want to be associated with me—especially since my case was connected to a battle with the RIAA. It was as if I was contagious or something. I tried to be brave and put on a good face: I showed up for an awards show, wearing a smile. But that smile belied a deep sorrow—a heartache that still hurts me to think about.

Even in the midst of all of that darkness, one person has always been an angel to me—Prince. Right after I filed for bankruptcy, he called. "Toni Braxton, how are you?" he asked. We hadn't ever met or even talked before that day—so his call came out of the blue. Yet a few seconds into the conversation, I knew we had a connection.

"I'm okay," I said. We both laughed a little because we knew that wasn't really the case.

"A while back, I told L.A. and Kenny this was going to happen," he said. "If you need anything from me, call me." His call that day still means so much to me—and he has continued to check in on me since.

Around this time, I'd already been dealing with another challenge. Rumors had long been circulating around LaFace that L.A. and Kenny had actually split. Their relationship had already shifted a few years earlier: In 1993, Kenny told the press that L.A. would oversee the ins and outs of the label's business side, and he would be focused on songwriting. Once when I accepted an award for "Breathe Again," I thanked both L.A. and Kenny for writing and producing such a beautiful song. Afterward, Tracey, Kenny's wife, called me up and said, "L.A. didn't write that song—Kenny did." "But even though Kenny wrote the song, L.A. produced it," I said. "That's why I thanked them both," I said. Some said the two had creative differences, while others said their disagreements were about money. Regardless, one thing was clear to me by 1998: They had gone in two different directions. In fact, they never seemed to be in the studio at the same time. So all in all, things were tense—it's always tough to watch two people you love fighting.

Though I'd sued LaFace, my dispute was never really with L.A. and Kenny; it was with Arista—which is why I was able to maintain at least a working relationship with both of them. L.A. and I never talked about the fact that he hadn't returned my calls in the weeks leading up to the bankruptcy—we just moved on. And by then, I'd realized that Arista had given L.A. and Kenny a deal that was nearly as crappy as mine.

AROUND THE TIME of the bankruptcy, my relationship with Curtis shifted. In general, he'd been very supportive and stood by me through the early weeks of the ordeal—but then things started to get weird in other ways. For instance, I was finding it tougher and tougher to understand some of his new restrictions on our physical touch. Yes, we'd agreed to save the ultimate act for marriage—but then he started saying things like, "We shouldn't touch each other below the neck." We'd be making out, and all of a sudden, he'd just stop. "That could lead to other things," he'd say. True—but at a time when my whole world was falling apart, I really needed his consolation, not more rules. And how could he really expect us to stay above the neck when we would sometimes sleep in the bed together when we visited each other? I was thinking, *Okay—if you don't want to make out below the neck, then you'd better go sleep in a separate bedroom.*

Curtis also started making statements like, "You're going through this bankruptcy because God wants you to get back with Him. He wants you to let go of all these materialistic things." I'm like, "What materialistic things?" It sounded crazy to me that God would somehow cause this bankruptcy—so I just chalked it up to Curtis not knowing what else to say or how to comfort me. We didn't really argue—yet when he made the kinds of statements he was making, it definitely drove a wedge between us. More and more, I noticed he seemed distant and moody. Even still, I knew I wanted to be with Curtis forever. Love does that to a girl.

A couple months after I filed for bankruptcy, I flew to Pittsburgh to spend time with Curtis—he said he needed to talk to me. I had a bad feeling in my stomach even before I boarded the plane. What he told me during that trip sends shivers up my spine: "Jesus told me we had to break up." I stared at him blankly. "What?" I finally managed to say. "God told me that we shouldn't be together anymore." No matter how I pressed him, he kept repeating what Jesus told him. It felt like he was breaking up with me using a one-liner on a Post-it note—and the fact that it was face-to-face made it all the more heart-wrenching. "I can best serve you as your friend," he finally added. Huh? "We're friends now," I protested. "We're not lovers—we haven't even been intimate!" But it was clear he'd already made his choice—and it's one that, to this day, I still don't really understand. I flew back to Los Angeles feeling numb and confused. I was completely heartbroken—there's just no other way to put it. Once home, I curled up in my bedroom and cried like a little kid—something I'd gotten used to during the bankruptcy.

Even with as much pain as I was in, I did my best to focus on my next chapter. I knew I had to somehow put the one-two punch of financial and relationship devastations behind me. I also knew I needed to get some money coming in—other than the $10,000 that Curtis had given me, I had no other income. I only used the money I did have on basics like food. By this time, because I'd already been declared bankrupt, I could at least earn new money—so work beckoned even more feverishly than it usually does for me.

Since I'd always wanted to try acting (and because it was a great way to earn income), I took a role on Broadway as Belle in *Beauty and the Beast* in September 1998. I rented a place on the Upper West Side of Manhattan. The show was exactly the change I needed: I was out of my element as a singer, so I had the opportunity to experiment with another form of artistry. I loved the gorgeous costume dresses (costume designer Ann Hould-Ward created an off-the-shoulder gown just for me!) as well as the energy of a live audience. And I considered it a great honor to be the first black actress to ever play Belle in the show. The most difficult part was the commute: On my off days, I flew from New York back to Los Angeles for the bankruptcy depositions. It was quite an exhausting schedule, yet I was grateful to be consumed by something other than the huge challenges I was facing.

Even still, I won't deny that I was seriously depressed as I did the show. I'm sure a lot of people were thinking, *She must be happy to be doing the show*—and I was. I could disappear into the performance, but as soon as the curtains closed and I dragged myself home, all I had the energy to do was climb into bed. Most of the time, I had this strange feeling that my body was vibrating—as if there was a constant heartbeat beneath every part of my skin. And I don't know why, but I ate a lot of cantaloupe. I would take the fruit, cut it in half, take out the seeds, and just sit there and eat it. For some reason, that's one of the only things that brought me a little relief every day. I never actually tried to take my life, but when I look back on that time, I think I might've been somewhat suicidal—for instance, I stopped being so careful when I crossed the street. I walked around New York like a zombie.

Mommy knew how down I was feeling—I didn't even have to tell her, because she could sense it. She's one of those people who knows how to offer others great comfort during times of crisis—any one of Mommy's friends can tell you that she's the one to call when you're feeling depressed. She is a spiritual life coach. "This too shall pass," she would remind me. "This is just a phase. It's seasonal. We do not claim this." I was particularly grateful for Mom's encouragement, I had few people to rely on. And forget a social life: I was much too embarrassed even to be seen. I was sure the whole world was thinking, *She's dumb. She's stupid. She's broke.* I wore a brave face during the Broadway show—but I mostly hid otherwise.

There were a few bright spots during that dark period: I received so much support from fans who'd heard about my financial struggles. Can you believe people actually sent me checks for $200 and $300? Jamie Foster Brown, the founder and editor of *Sister2Sister* magazine, even sent me a check. I never actually cashed the checks—but I appreciated each gesture of kindness.

For my six-month run in *Beauty and the Beast*, composer Alan Menken and lyricist Tim Rice wrote a new song for me to sing in the show. "A Change in Me" perfectly captures a pivotal moment for my character, Belle. "There's been a change in me, a kind of moving on," I sang in each performance. "Though what I used to be I still depend on. For now I realize that good can come from bad. That may not make me wise, but oh it makes me glad." A lyrical transformation for a princess—and a dramatic turning point for me.

CHAPTER 13

Battle Wounds

Here's what most people don't know: I won my bankruptcy case because of Kenny. Toward the end of the proceedings, the judge said to him, "You're an artist. If you were offered the amount of money that Toni was offered, would you have taken it?" Kenny paused. "No, I wouldn't," he said. L.A., who was in the courtroom that day, gave Kenny the look of death. I couldn't believe he said that—I will always love him for telling the truth in spite of his situation. By then, Kenny and I wanted exactly the same thing—to finally settle the case. His testimony is what helped to make that happen.

In January 1999, I finally reached an agreement with Arista and LaFace—and got a check for $20 million. I bought back my Grammys, designer dresses, and other valuables. In short, I won—but because the case left me so bloody, it didn't feel like as much of a victory as it should have. I'd hired lots of attorneys to represent me in what turned out to be a David versus Goliath battle. The RIAA and the record companies were lobbying against my case and trying to change the bankruptcy rules for all artists, so my lawyers had to get a lobbyist to lobby on my behalf; the RIAA's proposed legislation was eventually declared unconstitutional.

Yet even after that triumph, I couldn't tell the world the whole story because of a gag order. Upon settling, I had to sign an agreement ensuring that I would remain silent about the dollar figure of my payment for ten years. Let's just say that I couldn't be on the annual *Forbes* list because nobody could know how much I had received. So while I may have been privately exonerated, a certain public perception remained: Many still believed that I was broke.

The $20 million did allow me to start over. Because of the magnitude of my legal case, I had to pay millions in commissions and fees to my agents, managers, and attorneys. And of course, I handed over about $8 million for taxes. In the end, I was left with about $7 million, which I used to rebuild. I moved from L.A. to Atlanta and bought a home there. I set up a retirement account and bought some life insurance. At last, I was back on my feet—at least financially.

MEANWHILE, MY FRIENDSHIP with Keri, which had started during my Kenny G tour, began to blossom. We'd often spend hours together, writing music in the studio. "That's hot!" I'd tell Keri when he played a track for me. He was not only an amazing keyboardist—he was also a super-talented producer. In fact, in 2000, he left his band to work on my production team at LaFace. Keri's relationship with his girlfriend eventually ended, and once it did, we both slowly realized our connection was a little more than just a friendship (we'd been what I call "flirty friends" for at least a year . . .).

Early on, we never made anything official—we just knew there was a spark between us. But in 1999, while I was doing *Beauty and the Beast* in New York, we actually started dating. Our first real date was a movie. We went to see *The Best Man* starring Taye Diggs, Morris Chestnut, and Nia Long. I threw on my hat and scarf as a disguise—though I didn't really need to do that in a place like New York. And by the way, have I mentioned just how much I love the movies? *All About Eve* and *The Heiress* are two of my all-time faves. And I'm always amazed by the talents of my favorite actresses—Whoopi Goldberg and Meryl Streep. A movie was a perfect choice for a first date.

Keri was exactly what I needed at that time in my life—a calm spirit. Back in those days, Keri was a vegetarian. "You've gotta eat better," he would tell me. But I loved my meat. "I don't get it," I'd joke. "If you're going to eat cheese, you might as well eat beef—they're both from an animal." "They're different!" he'd say insistently. For years, he and most of the guys in Mint Condition had never touched meat—they used to be meat eaters, but they became vegetarians. Keri has always been so laid-back and cool. I'm exactly the opposite. "Count to eight until the rest of the world has caught up!" he'd often tease me. With all the craziness in my life—my parents' marital problems, the bankruptcy, the lawsuit—he made me slow down and just breathe. That was really the attraction. I'd call him up on the phone and we'd talk late into the night. With so much on my mind, I often had insomnia (most entertainers are control freaks—including me—and we're constantly trying to figure things out. A sleeping pill usually does nothing to get us to doze . . .). Keri and I would chat about silly stuff, like the latest movies. But little by little, I began confiding in him about personal things. Over time, we became emotionally and physically intimate.

I found out in between my Saturday-night show and my Sunday matinee of *Beauty and the Beast* that I was expecting. That Sunday morning, I'd asked my assistant to pick up an e.p.t. pregnancy test for me, but I lied and told him it was to play a practical joke on one of the cast members. He got the double pack, which was a good thing—because when it came up positive I immediately thought, *That couldn't be correct.* I shook the test stick like they used to do with the old mercury thermometers, hoping that the double line would go away. It didn't. So I drank forty ounces of water as a way to make my urine clear and dilute any traces of HCG, the hormone that signals pregnancy. Finally, I peed on the stick—and I got exactly the same result.

I kinda laughed at first—I guess I was just shocked. I hadn't been sexually active for at least a year and a half before

Keri, but I still considered myself a "safe-sex girl." As reality set in, I became really mad at myself. My mind went back to that one night when Keri and I had not used protection . . . but not quite the whole time. I worked up the nerve to call Keri and tell him the news—and his response immediately put me at ease. "We'll get through this together," he said, reassuring me. "Whatever you want to do, I'll support you." He was a complete gentleman who said all the right things—just like you hear in the movies. (Secretly, the performer in me was hoping for a little drama . . . not the Maury Povich show, but maybe an argument or a few tears.) Within a couple of hours of my call, Keri got on a plane and flew from Minnesota to New York just to be with me. I knew then that I would marry him someday.

When I discovered I was pregnant, I was right in the middle of a six-month prescription for Accutane—a kind of miracle drug for acne. I had begun taking it because all of the stresses of my life were showing up on my face. Like every drug, this one had its side effects. In fact, when my dermatologist gave me the prescription, I had to sign a waiver saying that if I got pregnant while on the drug, the fetus could be severely deformed—even two years after the prescription ended. But that didn't deter me, because I'd have done anything to get rid of my crunchy skin. So I scribbled my signature and got the prescription filled in ten minutes at a ma-and-pa pharmacist. I do remember seeing the pictures of a deformed baby on the back of the package, but I set it aside quickly. I couldn't wait for the day when my acne would magically disappear and I could be "cute" again. Within weeks, the Accutane began to work. But on the afternoon when I discovered I was pregnant, I was suddenly faced with a choice I'd never thought I'd have to make. Amid my major misgivings about abortion (according to my strict religious upbringing, God considers abortion wrong . . . so you can imagine how much agonizing I did), I eventually made a gut-wrenching decision—I would abort.

On the Monday following my test, I called my ob-gyn and told him my news. "I'm excited for you!" he said. I then told him I was planning to terminate the pregnancy—and he went dead silent. I could tell he was judging me. So before he could speak, I quickly added, "I'm on Accutane—and that's why I'm making this decision." The doctor seemed relieved once he heard my rationale, and his tone completely changed. But I knew that even if I weren't on the medication, I would've made the same decision. I felt selfish. I certainly wasn't wealthy, but I was rich enough to take care of a child—I'd just received that settlement check. My reasons had more to do with convenience than they did the fear that my baby would be abnormal. Yet I had them anyway.

The morning I showed up for my appointment, Keri came with me and stood by in the waiting room. He was the only person who knew what I was facing—I was too guilt-ridden to tell my family. I had the procedure done at Cedars-Sinai Hospital rather than in a clinic—because I'd been taking Accutane, my procedure had been deemed a "medical abortion" and therefore could take place in a hospital. When a nurse came in and looked over my chart, she said in a not-so-nice tone, "Oh—so you're having a D&E," which is a dilation and extraction—another term for an abortion. I sat there wishing the floor would open up and swallow me. When it came to my abortion being medically necessary, the nurse didn't mention that part—either to me or to the Mexican doctor who later came in to perform the procedure. I felt exposed—like everyone there knew my real reasons for having the abortion. It was as if I could hear the doctor thinking, You are a grown woman—and you can afford to have this baby. I sat there in total silence.

The anesthesiologist broke the tension with his light-hearted manner. "Do you like to cook?" he asked, prepping me to go under. I nodded and smiled. "Well, I've got a recipe for you," he said. "Here's how you can make a great sautéed shrimp." He then walked me through every step, laughing all the way through it—"You take a skillet, put a little olive oil in it, put in the shrimp, throw in some spices, add a little butter, some orange juice, and Grand Marnier, stir it, thicken it up a bit, and voilà!" Meanwhile, I was so pleasantly distracted from what I was there to do that I barely even remember the moment I was out.

When I awakened less than an hour later, I was throbbing . . . down there. Very sore, very crampy. I even bled a little. After spending another hour in a recovery room, I finally met Keri in the waiting lounge. We embraced without a word (Keri's calming presence was enough), and he helped me out to the car. Once we were back at the condo, I climbed into bed to rest. The following day, I woke up feeling so angry. *What did I do?* There was no easy answer to that question. The truth is that I'd made a choice that violated every religious principle I was raised to believe—and that reality suddenly overwhelmed me. I also felt that with everything I'd been given—a great relationship with Keri and an amazing career—I had little to show God for it. I felt like I'd taken advantage of the gifts He had given me—and that made me furious with myself. I felt like I deserved whatever I got.

For weeks after the abortion, I was in denial of how ashamed I felt. Though Keri continued to show me his support through his daily presence, he and I never really talked much about all the deep emotions I was experiencing. I just tried to move on as if nothing had happened and do what I've always done during difficult times—busy myself with work.

As I wrapped up my Broadway run, Disney offered me a role in *Beauty and the Beast* in London. I thought about it but decided it was time to go back to recording—and besides that, my record contract stated that I needed to begin recording immediately. So since I'd sorted out the mess with Arista, I signed another deal with LaFace and began on a third album. Yet whenever I would think about the decision I'd made, I would tell myself, "I had to do it. I had no choice." It's amazing how you can brainwash yourself into really believing something you know isn't true. Over the following months as my romance with Keri deepened, I would have that conversation with myself many, many times. In my heart, I believed I had taken a life—an action that I thought God might one day punish me for.

. . .

ONE NIGHT IN 1999, my father went out of the house to run an errand—and he left behind a green bag that he usually carried with him. Mommy was trying to find something, so she went searching in his bag. She ran across Daddy's phone bill, which listed one certain phone number several times. My mother somehow connected that phone number to an address—and a couple days later, she and my cousin Gilda drove to that home. The woman who answered the front door was the secretary of my father's boss at Baltimore Gas and Electric—that same woman my former assistant had seen him with at that concert. When Mommy asked the woman whether she was having an affair with Dad, the woman said, "Well, I'm glad you finally know."

That same day, my mother confronted my father—and Towanda, who was staying at the house then, called me as it happened. "Mommy and Daddy are arguing like crazy!" she said. Since I wasn't actually there, I don't know what kind of angry words were exchanged or whether my parents ever resolved anything. Within days, my parents separated.

My siblings and I were livid. We all tried to get the woman on a conference call, but she hung up when she heard Towanda's question: "Are you messing around with my father?" Of course, Dad was angry with us for calling the woman—but he couldn't have been as furious as I was with him. Eventually, the whole story came out. My father—the reverend who promised to be faithful to my mother and to honor his vow before

God—had been carrying on an affair with his coworker for nine years.

There was brief talk of a reconciliation between my parents—but the wound was too deep. Once their lawyers reached an agreement, Mommy and Daddy divorced—and thirty days later, my father married his mistress. The whole ordeal sent me into an emotional tailspin. It made me question every single thing I'd ever been taught—about God, about religion, about ethics. It was the most confusing and painful time I've ever experienced. And through it all, one person stood by me—Keri.

CHAPTER 14

"Life Is Not a Fairy Tale"

I spent Christmas with Keri. It was snowing the day I flew into Minneapolis in December 1999—but that didn't matter to me because I was with the man I'd grown to love. On Christmas Eve, we went out shopping and then to dinner. "You should get your nails done," Keri said, prodding me. The following day, his nudging would make perfect sense.

Late on Christmas morning, the two of us dragged ourselves out of bed and into the living room to open our gifts. Still wearing my pajamas (a pair with little teacups all over them), I sat right in front of the lighted tree. I reached for a present Keri had gotten me and unwrapped it. Inside, I found a skirt, one that I could immediately see was too long for me. "Thanks!" I said, forcing a smile—but I'm sure Keri could tell I wasn't very impressed. His other two gifts were better—more sets of PJs (I can never have too many!) and a pair of cozy slippers. Once my gifts were all open, I went to the restroom for a couple minutes. When I returned, Keri was down on one knee—and holding a Tiffany box. "Will you marry me?" he said. I froze. I hadn't seen this coming at all.

My thoughts raced. *Do I even want to get married? Am I really over Curtis? And is this the right choice?* Realizing that my hesitation had made the moment awkward, I kinda hugged Keri—yet I didn't really give an answer. "So is that a yes?" he finally said, chuckling. "Yes," I said—but to be honest, I still wasn't 100 percent sure.

My uncertainty had little to do with Keri. When I had met him, I was still getting over that heartbreak with Curtis—and I was torn about whether he and I should get back together. I'd eventually moved on and started a relationship with Keri, of course, but I did so with a question mark: Could Curtis and I work things out? I thought I'd settled that—but the day Keri asked me to marry him, the question resurfaced.

It surprised even me that I didn't give an immediate yes to Keri. We'd been together for just a bit, and for the previous few months, I'd been telling myself, "I'm going to break up with him if he doesn't propose by Valentine's Day." We'd talked a little about marriage, and we'd once even gone to Tiffany to look at rings. And we'd already survived a major experience together—a pregnancy. Plus, I also think it's nonsense to date someone for a long time—I'm sure that has a lot to do with my traditional upbringing. So I knew I loved Keri and that I wanted to marry him. Yet when I saw him down on one knee in front of the Christmas tree, I suddenly wasn't sure.

Keri and I never talked about my hesitation—and that day, I tucked it away in some secret chamber of my heart. Keri took the ring out of the box and slid it onto my ring finger. It was a diamond solitaire with clusters of smaller diamonds around it in a raised setting. "It's nice," I said. As I looked down at the ring on my hand, I suddenly wished that I'd responded to Keri's suggestion and gotten that manicure—my polish was chipped.

"You have to ask my dad if you can marry me," I told Keri.

So right away, Keri called my father. "I just proposed to your daughter and she said yes," he told my dad. "Do I have your permission to marry her?" My father agreed. Both my parents, who'd gotten to know Keri by that time, seemed excited. Later, I called my manager, Barry Hankerson, and told him the news. "Congratulations!" he said. On Christmas night, Keri pinched a nerve in his back and could hardly move, but once he was back on his feet the next day, we drove over to his parents' home in Saint Paul and told them the news. We all celebrated.

BY THE TIME Kenny and I got back in the studio to start on my third album, he and L.A. had officially split, even though they did still write and produce some material together. In 2000, the two sold their share of LaFace to BMG, Arista's parent company, which meant that I and the other LaFace artists would be transferred to BMG/Arista. Clive Davis left to start J Records, which was funded by BMG. L.A. succeeded Clive as chairman and CEO of Arista. I'd relied so heavily on L.A. and Kenny's Batman and Robin duo, and without it, I was nervous about putting out a record. They were still friendly with one another—and even after his promotion, L.A. provided plenty of direction in my career. But it didn't feel like the early days when I'd had the magic of the team behind me. And though the bankruptcy had been settled by the time we started the third album, some of the war wounds still felt fresh—that was the elephant in the room that nobody wanted to mention. We'd mainly agreed to collaborate on a third album because the BMG execs wanted to get their money's worth on our contractual agreement. And with the news of the bankruptcy still hanging over my name, it's not like others in the industry were clamoring to pull me away to work with them.

Though my lawsuit with the label was settled, relationships had shifted. Before the legal drama, I'd often been invited to BMG parties or asked to sing at charity functions. Those invitations stopped. Execs used to request favors from me, like "Toni, can you sing at the billionaires' club reception?" Not anymore. I was no longer the flavor-of-the-month artist, and while no one actually acknowledged it verbally, I could feel the tension in the air. I also felt that there was less enthusiasm about me and my music.

L.A. sent me a track that he thought would be perfect for my album—it was called "He Wasn't Man Enough for Me." When he sent me the track, which was by Rodney Jerkins, I loved it, but didn't get the chorus. "Where's the hook?" I said after he played it. "You don't hear it until like a minute and twenty-eight seconds into the song."

L.A. shrugged. "I think it's hot," he said insistently. L.A. could talk me into anything. "Just try it." I did—and once I rehearsed and eventually recorded the tune, it became one of my favorites. It was a switch from all those sad love songs on my first couple of albums. The fast tempo and lyrics made it so fun to sing.

Keri was in the studio with me a lot—and L.A. obviously approved. "That's the one right there," he'd often say when he'd see Keri around the studio. "He's such a talented producer. You're with the right guy." He and I would spend hours together, just listening to tracks. There's something so intimate about working with someone on a creative project. That's probably why so many people who work together end up liking each other.

Barry Hankerson had become my manager during the bankruptcy and my parents' divorce. Especially after L.A. left LaFace and moved up the ladder at Arista, Barry took on an even bigger role in my career. From the start, I thought he was brilliant—one of the smartest managers, producers, and entertainment lawyers I'd ever met. He also knew his way around the music world: He was once married to Gladys Knight, he'd worked closely with the Winans, and he managed R. Kelly and his niece, Aaliyah, through his label, Blackground. He entered my life at a time when I was feeling powerless. "You're going to be all right," he would often tell me. "You may not sell what you used to sell, but you're going to make a comeback. You'll be bigger than ever."

My third album, *The Heat,* debuted in April 2000. Not only did "Man Enough," the first single released, have a different sound, a lot of the record was more urban and upbeat. "Gimme Some," one of the tracks, features a rap from TLC's Lisa "Left Eye" Lopes. Keri and I teamed up to write and produce the song's title track, "The Heat," a sexy, mid-tempo groove that celebrates the electricity that connects two would-be lovers. And just so it could be called a Toni Braxton album, I had to include at least a couple slow songs about romance gone sour—and "Just Be a Man About It" was one such hit.

Once the album was released, Barry sent me out on a radio tour. "You've got to pay homage to radio so that they'll continue to want to play your music," he told me. At the time, that made sense to me: It's important for an artist to stop in and say hello to DJs so that she stays on the radar. But L.A. thought this was the wrong strategy for an established artist—and he told me that. "Why is Toni Braxton doing radio tours?" he asked me. "Barry is just using you to sell records and keep relationships for his other artists." The record business is a business of payoffs and favors—so a manager will often say to a radio station, "If your station sponsors Toni Braxton's tour, I will give you another artist's album early." So L.A. believed that Barry was sending me out to radio stations in exchange for more airtime for his niece and his other artists. This is just one example of how L.A. and Barry disagreed—and I usually felt caught in the middle of their power struggles.

I had no idea whether *The Heat* would be well received— as an artist, you're always hoping that people will embrace your music. But with a lawsuit, a bankruptcy, and a corporate restructuring in the news in the previous few years, it was hard for me to tell whether the record would do well. That's why I'll always be so thankful that my fans really got behind me: *The Heat* eventually sold well and even brought me my sixth Grammy. No, it didn't catch on the way my first two albums did (each sold more than ten million copies around the world), but it still sold six million copies worldwide. Sweet redemption—that's the best way to describe how it felt. The album's success was proof that the world could look beyond the headlines—and that I could finally turn the page on one of my most agonizing chapters.

AFTER KERI AND I got engaged, I had a house built in Atlanta using the money I received from the bankruptcy settlement. Soon after, we hired Diann Valentine as our wedding planner and chose a date—April 21, 2001. That gave us enough time to pull together all the details: the venue, the ceremony, the flowers, the guest list, the music, and, of course, the dress. I chose Davett Singletary (my longtime colleague at LaFace who'd become a beloved friend) as my maid of honor. And of course, all my sisters were in the wedding—each was a bridesmaid. By then, a couple of my sisters had made their own trips to the altar: Traci and Trina had both exchanged vows. When I told my sisters that Keri and I were finally ready to tie the knot, each seemed genuinely happy for me. We Braxton sisters have always shown up to support one another. That's just how we roll in our family.

I told Diann the color I'd already chosen for the wedding—Tiffany blue. Who knew that Tiffany owns the patent to Tiffany blue? Thankfully, Diann negotiated a deal for us to be able to use the color. As for my dress, I fell in love with an ivory, strapless Vera Wang gown. On the most special day of my life, I wanted to feel like a princess—and that's exactly how I felt the first time I put on that gown.

My road to the altar was littered with family drama—it wouldn't be a Braxton family event if there wasn't at least one crazy incident. In October 2000, my parents' divorce became final—which meant Mommy and Daddy wanted nothing to do with each other. They wouldn't even agree to share a table at the wedding. Mommy wanted to bring the gentleman friend she'd been dating. Absolutely not. Then Dad asked me if he could bring his new wife. Hell no. My father even threatened not to come to my wedding if his new bride couldn't accompany him, but I stood my ground. He finally decided to come on his own, which is a good thing—because if my father had shown up at my wedding with that woman, the two of them would've been promptly escorted out.

Several weeks before the wedding, I visited the dermatologist. "You're breaking out a little," he said, examining my face. "Looks hormonal." Then a week before the wedding, I went to my primary care physician for a general checkup. "So you're getting married," he said. "Are you planning to have kids right away?" I nodded and smiled. "Well, you're getting an early start—you're pregnant now." I just stared at him. As it turns out, I wasn't very far along—in fact, I hadn't even missed a period. I'd had a few headaches and some nausea, which I attributed to the stress of planning the wedding. But when the doctor checked my cervix, he noticed that it was purple—which is a sign of pregnancy. That's when he gave me a pregnancy test that confirmed that I was expecting.

My big day finally arrived. I think my mother forgot that it was my wedding—she was still so angry with my father that her energy was negative. "Life is not a fairy tale," she told me as I put on my gown. "All men cheat." She did give me a gift—she'd turned her own wedding ring into a gorgeous bracelet. "I hope this brings you more luck than it brought me," she said as she fastened it onto my wrist. Even though I knew she said these words because she cared for me, her words still hurt me.

At Dean Gardens in Atlanta, the guests gathered—among them were Tyler Perry, Usher, TLC, Kenny, and dozens of my extended family members. Some of my father's sisters didn't show up—I invited them, of course, but that word somehow hadn't gotten to my father. My parents' divorce was so recent that the entire family was still reeling from it—so I'm sure that had something to do with the miscommunication.

Andrew Young, the former mayor of Atlanta, officiated the ceremony. I had a few jitters, but I was more excited than nervous as my father took my hand and walked me down the aisle. Saying my vows—"I, Toni Braxton, take you, Keri Lewis, to be my lawfully wedded husband"—felt like an out-of-body experience. *Me? Married?* I'd always imagined I'd stand at the altar and profess my love for the man I'd chosen, but I just couldn't believe the moment had actually come. The ceremony itself was perfect—as magical as I'd dreamed it would be. There's just one thing I wished I would've added— the traditional broom-jumping ceremony. It would've been nice to pass the broom on to my children.

Keri and I stole a private moment for ourselves right after the ceremony. I handed him something I'd brought with me—a rattle.

"What's this?" he asked, taking the rattle.

I smiled. "Well," I said, "you're going to be a daddy."

"Really?!" he exclaimed, his eyes brightening. "Wow," he finally said, "this is the happiest day of my life." We embraced. The news of my pregnancy was the greatest gift I could've given either one of us—both on that day and for many, many years to come.

CHAPTER 15

Leaks, Lies, and Revelations

I was terrified the first time I held my son. He'd just been delivered by C-section, and I was so drugged that I could hardly sit up straight. I also still had the shakes from the epidural. But my mother made me hold him right away. "You have to bond with your baby," she said. Most of my family was there with me at the hospital—only my brother, Mikey, hadn't been able to make it, because of work responsibilities. "I don't think he looks like me," I said, glancing over at Keri as I struggled to embrace our beloved bundle. My lower eyelids filled with water. "What's wrong?" asked Keri, noticing my tears. I didn't really give him an answer. But looking back on it, I think I was overwhelmed by the thought that I was suddenly responsible for the life of this little child. On December 2,

2001, just eight months after I'd married, I became a mother—to the healthy and handsome Denim Cole Braxton-Lewis.

There have been moments when I felt more like my son's big sister than his mom. That's probably because I spent all those years coparenting my younger siblings, and being in the role of caretaker brings back all those memories. And yet right from the start, my connection with Denim was so much deeper than the bond often shared between siblings—I would do absolutely anything for my child. I definitely felt that protective mother instinct when I held him. On the day Keri and I brought Denim home from the hospital, our hearts were wide open. Having a child gave me the capacity to love more unconditionally than I ever had.

Becoming a new parent was much harder than I thought it would be. I mean, I read every book you could think of to prepare for it—but I still didn't get it, even though I would call my own Mommy every day. Nobody tells you that no matter how much planning you do, it really comes down to on-the-job training. I remember not knowing what to do when Denim would spit up—and I certainly didn't know how to care for his umbilical cord stump before it fell off and became a navel. I also couldn't differentiate his cries: Was he colicky or hungry? And I don't even want to think back on the day he received his first set of shots—I cried just about as much as he did.

I hardly even had a chance to settle into my new role as mother before I began work on my fourth studio album—my contract stipulated that I needed to begin work on my next project within a certain amount of time from my previous one. I could see that my sister Tamar really wanted to have a recording career—and I respected her drive—so I found a way to include her as a songwriter and background vocalist on several of the album's songs. Aside from that move, little else about the album reflected my choices—I was simply following the directions of the people around me. Everyone seemed to want to give me a younger, more hip-hop sound.

My manager, Barry, hired the hip-hop and R&B producer Irv Gotti to work with me—at the time, Irv was very hot and had some hits. Irv was very expensive—about $250,000 a song—and the record's whole budget was $2 million. When L.A. heard Barry was using him, he had a fit. "Why are we paying Irv top-shelf?" he asked. He still believed that Barry was trying to use me for the benefit of his own label. "A Toni Braxton record is already going to sell at least five hundred thousand units." But Barry insisted it was the right decision. "You need to switch things up and appeal to a younger audience," he told me. "Working with Gotti will be a good thing. You should do a little hip-hop here and there. It's going to be hot." Once again, I was caught between two bickering men—and suppressing my opinion in order to keep the peace.

Yet Barry wasn't the only one who wanted to change my musical style—even L.A. seemed to be trying to redefine me. "I've already had upbeat songs like 'You're Makin' Me High' and 'Man Enough,' " I reminded L.A. But even still, he wanted me to include some sprinkles of hip-hop. That's why L.A. wanted to include tracks like "Hit the Freeway"—which he picked R&B producer and tastemaker Pharrell to write.

I'm a big Pharrell fan, and I liked the beat of the song. But he didn't seem all that concerned about how my vocals sounded (even if I hit a wrong note, he kept it in!)—he was more focused on the emotion of the track. "I don't want to do songs like 'Hit the Freeway,' " I told him. "It doesn't feel like me. I'm not a rapper."

"You have to stay ahead of the curve," L.A. kept telling me. "You see how Usher was ahead of the curve when the whole dance explosion hit?" But Usher is a male artist—and male artists can usually take more risks than female artists can. Of course I wanted to stay fresh and relevant—but I also wanted to stay true to my DNA. Even still, I allowed the voices of those managing me to drown out my opinion.

L.A. had just signed Robert Smith (who was then with Brandy) as a producer, so he also wanted me to work with Robert—so the whole album was very political. And not only was there a constant tug-of-war between Barry and L.A., but Clive and L.A. were often at odds. I felt like I was being tossed in every direction, trying to please both my record company and my management. And in the meantime, I did nothing to please myself.

Just as I was gearing up for the album's release, I discovered that I was pregnant. Again. I was horribly sick with nausea—I could barely even keep down a cracker and a glass of soda water—and the doctor even put me on bed rest. The doctor also discovered that my placenta had become detached. The worst part of the situation is that when I asked the Arista execs if we could postpone my record by a few months, Barry told me that they refused—which I later wondered about. So *More Than a Woman* came out on November 19, 2002—and from the start, it was a disaster. I consider it the worst album I've done. Ever. It's like that one-night stand you just don't want to talk about.

Even before the record hit, there was drama: "No More Love" was leaked (the track, which sampled Luther Vandross's song "Never Too Much," was supposed to be our second single; the first was to be "Hit the Freeway"). But since "No More Love" was already out there, Arista decided not to include it on the final record. So my first single instead turned out to be "Hit the Freeway"—and it was the weakest debut of my career. It peaked at number eighty-six on the *Billboard* Hot 100 chart.

Things went downhill from there: The album didn't catch on all that well. And with such a complicated pregnancy, I'd had no energy to fight with the record company—or to get out and really promote the new music once the album was finished. That's exactly why I'd asked Arista to delay it so I could give birth first.

On March 31, 2003, my second son arrived—and yes, he was delivered by C-section, too. We named him Diezel Ky Braxton-Lewis. People often ask me how I came up with my sons' names. Denim was originally supposed to be Denham. But in the hospital when I heard a nurse say, "How's little Den Ham?" I decided right then and there that I needed to change the spelling to "Denim," like the jeans, so that people would know how to pronounce it. Keri is half-German, and we wanted to celebrate that heritage with our second son's name. So we named him after Rudolf Diesel, the German engineer who invented the diesel engine. We changed the "s" to a "z" just to personalize it.

Around this time, my manager Barry called me up one afternoon. "I've got some bad news for you, Toni," he said. "L.A.'s about to drop you from the label."

"What are you talking about?" I said.

"You're just not selling as well as you need to sell," he told me. I was stunned—in fact, I didn't even respond.

I thought about Barry's words over the next few days. Why would L.A. drop me without even talking to me about it? I was shocked that there was talk of dropping after just one flopped album—usually an artist gets two flops. I knew just one way to get a definite answer—and that was to ask L.A. myself. So I called L.A. directly. But what was true during the bankruptcy became true in this situation—he just didn't respond. I then tried to get some answers from Kenny—and he said he'd heard that Barry was telling Arista that I wanted to be off the label. But to be honest, I wasn't quite sure what to believe.

In the meantime, Barry continued whispering his warnings. "Arista is done with you," he said. "It's time for you to move on." No matter how many times he repeated that, I found it hard to believe. Yet because L.A. had gone completely silent on me—and because my latest album had done pretty poorly—I started to think that Barry might be telling me the truth. "If you left Arista, I could get you signed on to another label right away," Barry said, trying to persuade me. "You can make a comeback, Toni." So in April 2003, I took a bold step: I left BMG and Arista.

At first, Barry claimed that he was shopping me around to different labels—and yet strangely, I wasn't getting any calls or meetings. "Because of the bankruptcy," he explained, "no one wants to touch you." But after a few weeks, he stopped talking about other record companies and began playing up his own. "I'll sign you," he told me. "I know exactly how to promote your career. You should stick with me." At a time when I was already feeling so confused and vulnerable amid a bankruptcy, I trusted him. So in the spring of 2003 I signed with Barry and Blackground Records.

CHAPTER 16

Dangerous Liaison

"Can I finish the show?" is not the question you'd expect to hear from an actress who has just collapsed. Yet during a September 2003 performance of *Aida* on Broadway, that's exactly what I asked just before I was raced off to a hospital. Never mind that I'd just passed out—all I could think about was whether I would get through the show's last half. Let me explain.

I'm a workhorse—always have been. Less than three months after I gave birth to Diezel—and a few weeks after I left Arista—I took a leading role in *Aida* at New York's Palace Theatre. As our family's primary breadwinner, I knew I needed to get back to work. I'd enjoyed my run in *Beauty and the Beast,* so I thought I'd give acting another try. So even though I'd felt a little pressure in my chest during Diezel's birth—the same feeling I had back when I had asthma as a girl—I thought my asthma was just returning. So I dismissed the feeling and went right back to work.

One evening, I raced backstage to put on my costume for the last song of the first half before intermission. As I was stepping into a dress that my wardrobe stylist had ready for me, I began feeling light-headed—and then suddenly, everything went black. Out of the corner of his eye, the stage manager saw my whole body slump over onto my stylist. I lay against her, limp and lifeless—and then a few seconds later, my eyelids shot open. As if nothing had happened, I stood straight up. "Oh my God, I almost fell!" I said to the manager. He and the stylist were standing at my side with worried looks on their faces—and I was trying to figure out why.

"Toni, you didn't just feel that?" said the stage manager. "You fainted."

I stared at him blankly. "I didn't faint!" I said insistently. "I just slipped a little."

"No, you fell," he said. "I saw you."

I was so out of it that I hadn't even realized I'd collapsed—and I pressed the manager to let me continue getting dressed. "Can I just complete the show?" I pleaded. "I think I can finish."

He barely even let me get that statement all the way out before he cut in: "Absolutely not, Toni. No way. You fainted. Either you go to the hospital now yourself, or we're calling an ambulance." I definitely didn't want them to call an ambulance because then word would get out about my episode—so a moment later, I hopped into the backseat of a black sedan, and a driver sped me off to Lenox Hill Hospital on Manhattan's Upper East Side.

In the ER, I rushed right in to see the doctor. "What are your symptoms?" he asked.

"I just felt light-headed," I said, "and I was told that I fainted—but I don't remember it." I then explained that I'd been having chest pains for the previous couple weeks.

"Let's do an EKG," he said. I did the electrocardiogram—and then the nurse came in and told me that the doctor also needed me to do an echocardiogram, which is an ultrasound of my heart.

"Is everything okay?" I asked the nurse.

She paused. "The doctor will be with your shortly," she said—and the moment I heard that, I knew there must be a problem.

A half hour later, once the results were in, the doctor came to my room. "Miss Braxton," he said, "you have pericarditis."

My bottom lip trembled. "What's that?" I said.

"Essentially, you caught a virus that attacked your heart." He went on to explain that the condition is an inflammation of the pericardium, the sac that surrounds the heart.

"What causes it?" I asked.

"Many things can cause it," he explained. "We want you to stay a few days so we can monitor your particular case."

"But I can only stay one night because I have a show to do," I said in protest.

He reluctantly agreed—and when he released me the next day, he sent me off with many prescriptions. "I want you to see a specialist," the doctor told me. "I think lupus could be causing your pericarditis."

My eyes widened. "What is lupus?" I asked. I'd heard of the condition before, but I really didn't know much about it.

"Lupus is an autoimmune disorder in which the body attacks itself." That sounded scary—but I consoled myself with the thought that the doctor's theory wasn't a definite diagnosis.

The following day, I returned to the show. Because I was on, like, eight hundred milligrams of Motrin every eight hours, plus steroids and anti-inflammatory drugs and a lot of other medications that made me drowsy, I could barely keep my eyes open from scene to scene. After a week of that exhaustion, I did as the doctor instructed and went to check in with a specialist. She ran more tests—but none of them came up positive for lupus. And because the first doctor had already started treating my pericarditis, my body's inflammation started to go down. "The tests don't show it," she says, "but I believe you have lupus. If you were my sister, I would give you a prescription for Plaquenil."

"Really?" I said. "I don't want to take a drug if I'm not sure I have lupus."

She understood that—so just to gather a bit more evidence, she ordered a series of tests including an ANA (antinuclear antibodies) test, which can show whether someone has an autoimmune disorder. My ANA test came back positive. "You have two symptoms of lupus—pericarditis and a positive ANA test," the doctor told me. "I usually need three or four to make a diagnosis—but I still suspect you have lupus."

For the next several weeks, I put that news in the back of my head so I could focus—I needed to finish my show. Toward the end of the show's run in November, the specialist called me again. "I really think you should start on the Plaquenil," she said insistently. I did—but I wanted a second opinion on whether I really needed it. So once I returned to Los Angeles, I went to my own primary care physician, Dr. Young, who referred me to another specialist. That doctor ran yet another round of tests. "Stop taking that Plaquenil immediately," he told me. "Plaquenil is an antimalarial medication—and you don't need to be on that for any reason. Your tests do not show you have lupus."

I was relieved. "So what could be the cause of my symptoms?" I asked him.

"I'm not sure yet," he said. "But let's just keep testing you every six months and we'll find out whether you really have the condition." Over the next few years, I did as he suggested. And every single test came back with the exact same result— no lupus.

NOT VERY LONG into my time at Blackground Records, Barry's label, I knew I'd made a mistake—a major one. "Now that I'm on your label," I told Barry one morning, "you can't also be my manager." We'd already agreed on that when we'd signed the record contract—but apparently, he'd forgotten.

"What do you mean, Toni?" he said. "Of course I can still manage you!"

But I wouldn't give in on that point. So despite his disapproval, I brought in my own person, which made things tense. Barry did not want to work with anyone. Various people in the industry eventually came to me with stories of what Barry was telling Arista behind the scenes and how they thought that I had wanted to leave the label all along. Once I'd already left Arista, I received a FedEx package that provided one more small piece of evidence that Arista had never really been trying to get rid of me. In it was a square note card with a single line written across it: "I will always love you." It was from L.A.

Barry was smart, and starting from the time when he managed me at Arista, he'd taught me a lot. I learned just how much of a dollars-and-cents business the music industry really is. He even taught me how to read people—and how to read between the lines. And though I knew he could sometimes be difficult to work with, it became more apparent once I signed with him. I didn't make any immediate plans to leave Barry—but after some time, I knew I had to figure out how to break away from him. I had no idea how to even begin doing that.

Even I find it hard to believe that I actually enjoyed working on my fifth album. With so much negativity swirling around my relationship with Barry, you'd think that would've ruined the experience—but for a lot of it, I had my husband at my side. Keri continued to work as one of my producers, and the two of us teamed up on many of the songs. Barry actually let me pick my songs (at last . . . some artistic freedom!), and the tracks included a couple of my favorite tunes—"Please," "Trippin' (That's the Way Love Works)," and an acoustic ballad I still love called "Shadowless." During the time when we were making the album, I had a studio in my home, so Keri and I did a lot of our work from there. I even got to collaborate with Jimmy Jam and Terry Lewis (one of the hottest R&B and pop songwriting and production duos around). But because an issue arose over their payment, the songs we worked on didn't actually make it onto the album. Even still, I was proud of our effort—and I felt "Libra" really reflected my musical taste.

While I was at work on my album in 2004, Tyler Perry invited me to a screening of the first movie he'd produced for the big screen, *Diary of a Mad Black Woman,* which was still being edited. Afterward, he pulled me aside. "I would love for you to be on the movie soundtrack," he told me. I've always loved Tyler—after one of L.A.'s assistants introduced us to each other, we clicked at hello!—so I said, "Yes, let's talk about how we can work on something." So Keri, the songwriter Cory Rooney, and I created a track called "Stupid," which is a song about regret from a past relationship. At the end of the song, I sing, "Stupid is as stupid does, I'm stupid for you, baby, just because"—a lyric inspired by *Forrest Gump.*

When the track was finished, I sent it to Tyler. "I have

to have this song!" he called to tell me. "Toni Braxton, you actually said, 'Stupid is as stupid does'!" We both cracked up.

"Okay, then let's do it on the soundtrack," I said. "But let me run it by Blackground first."

I did that—and Barry gave me the go-ahead. "Barry, maybe my whole album should be the soundtrack for Tyler's movie," I suggested to him one afternoon. "That would be hot—kinda like Stevie Wonder did with *Woman in Red.*"

But Barry didn't like that idea. "Why would I split the profits of my blood, sweat, and tears with someone else?" Two days before *Diary of a Mad Black Woman* debuted in theaters on February 5, 2005, a rep from Lionsgate, the film's distribution company, called Barry to check in. Barry asked them to take me off the soundtrack. Barry had given the green light, of course—but he hadn't actually signed the paperwork. But the film was already sent to the theaters. Later, Tyler called me directly. "I talked to your uncle," he said. My siblings and I used to call my manager "Uncle Barry" because he'd become like a family member during those years when he'd helped me through the bankruptcy.

"I am so sorry, Tyler," I said. "I really do want to be part of your soundtrack." We chatted for a couple more minutes—but I knew that our relationship had been damaged beyond repair. In the end, Barry had to agree to let Tyler and Lionsgate keep the song in the movie because there were letters of intent that could prove he'd okayed the deal.

My record, *Libra,* was released on September 27, 2007— and though "Stupid" is played briefly in the movie, and the track is on my album, the song is not on the film's soundtrack. Now you know why. In the years after that incident, my friendship with Tyler eventually faded.

ON MY ONLY record with Blackground, my sales were horrible—surprise, surprise. With hardly any promotion from the label and with a sour relationship between Barry and me, none of the three singles really caught on. The album did eventually sell nearly seven hundred thousand copies and reached gold status—which might be good for some artists, but that's considered a failure for a singer whose previous records have sold in the millions. It's a miracle that it even sold one copy in the midst of so much drama.

At a time when I should've been heading into my peak years as a musician, I'd instead found myself on the set of a western shoot-'em-up movie. For the sake of my family, my career, I knew I had to break ties with "Uncle Barry"—and fast.

CHAPTER 17

A Motherly Instinct

Gladys Knight helped get me my Vegas show. We've known each other forever—back in the day, my sister Tamar even went to the prom with her son. She's like my auntie in the music business. So when I called her up and told her I wanted to get a show at the Flamingo—which is where she was just wrapping up a long run—Gladys put in a good word for me (the venue directors do a very extensive background check on new acts). "The Flamingo is a good house," Gladys assured me. "I think you'll do well there." My goal was to start at the Flamingo and then move over to a larger venue—the Mirage.

"Doing Vegas will age you," others told me. I disagreed. That's an old way of thinking, because Vegas now has a newer, younger face. And besides that, I've always kept a list of all the experiences I'd like to have during my lifetime, and a Vegas show had been on my list for a long time—so I was determined to make it happen.

The Flamingo's directors and my agents and I worked out a contract—I was to do five shows a week, and then there'd be a dark house on Sundays and Mondays. The room I had to fill was small by Vegas standards—about twelve hundred seats. For me, that was actually a great size, because I wanted to sell out: The smaller the room, the more likely you are to sell out . . . and when you fill every seat consistently, you're a better candidate for a bigger house. One of the hardest rooms to fill is the one built at the Colosseum for Céline Dion when she did her show with the director of Cirque du Soleil—it has 4,500 seats. But unlike my room, hers could be shared—the MGM Grand brought in Elton John to perform his show *The Red Piano* so she could take off a few months. There would be no time off for me.

My deal with the Flamingo was similar to the kind of deal I'd make with a record company during a tour: I was the producer for the show, and the Flamingo provided me with front-end money. Once that advance money was recouped through revenue from ticket sales, we'd split the profits. Artists who do well during their first couple years in Vegas can negotiate for a larger percentage of the profits—that's how some end up earning $20 million or more a year. Not a bad living. It was also the perfect arrangement for someone like me—a mother who wanted to stay in town with her children. As my family's main provider, I needed to work, but I didn't want to tour. A Vegas show made stability possible for us

Once I got to the Nevada desert, I had just two weeks to rehearse before the show's premiere—I was replacing Wayne Newton, who was just leaving, and the house directors never like to stay dark for long. As usual, Keri did all my sound production and helped me manage the show. My preview night was on May 19, 2006—and to be honest, it didn't go so well. We had a couple technical glitches (the sound went out . . . and I was still getting used to singing in such dry desert air, which affects many singers who perform in Vegas). I wished I'd had longer to rehearse—but I didn't want to risk losing my spot at the Flamingo. So I forged ahead with creating a show I called *Toni Braxton: Revealed.*

The show was a cabaret-style performance—which means I spent lots of money on lights, costumes, and set design. The whole thing was very Vegas cabaret: I wore a sexy black number (a sparkly body suit that I paired with a tuxedo jacket and fishnet stockings), I sang several of my most well-known songs, and I incorporated lots of interaction with the audience. I often called people up onstage and had them sing along with me—which taught me how to quickly read personalities and ad-lib. Throughout the ninety-minute show, I did seven costume changes; for the finale, I started with a slow version of "Un-Break My Heart" and then moved to an upbeat dance version. After a quick costume change (yes, another one!), I came out in a red dress and struck the same pose I was shown in on the front of the Flamingo building. The show was a lot of work—but it was also a whole lot of fun. And I absolutely loved it when other entertainers would drop by: Magic and Cookie Johnson once came through, and Nicole Murphy and Michael Strahan were regulars. Half of the time, I wouldn't know they were there until after the show—the blinding stage lights make it hard to see faces in the audience.

A few months into the show, my family came to see me perform—and Tamar wasn't impressed with the background singers. Mommy offered a great solution: "Maybe you should put your sisters in." I did. And though I knew that could mean a little drama, it was always comforting to have my family close by; and besides that, they always sound incredible.

First, it was Tamar and Trina who moved to Vegas to be background singers for about a year—and then it was Trina and Towanda. And finally, it was Towanda and Sparkle, who was then on R. Kelly's label, Rockland Records. In addition to my two background singers, I hired ten dancers—one of whom was Casper Smart, the dancer who, years later, dated Jennifer Lopez.

I ENROLLED BOTH of my sons in preschool—in the fall of 2006, Denim was four and Diezel was three. One October morning a few weeks after I'd enrolled them, I dropped them off and gave them each a good-bye kiss. About three that afternoon when I was rehearsing at the Flamingo, I got a call.

"Hello—Mrs. Braxton?"

"Yes?"

"This is the principal at your sons' school."

I pressed the cell right to my ear so I could hear every word the woman was saying. "Is everything okay?"

"Well," she said, "we need you to come pick up Diezel. He should not be at this school—we cannot facilitate his needs here."

"What do you mean?" I asked.

"Please come to the school and we'll talk about it," she said. I hung up, gathered my things, and went straight there. During the ten-minute drive, I could feel my hands trembling as I gripped the steering wheel.

At the school, the dean said that Diezel didn't have the kind of social skills that a child of his age would normally have. "What do you mean?" I asked. "We just can't facilitate his needs here," she repeated. She said he wasn't bothering the other kids—in fact, it was the opposite. He was staying off to himself and not mixing with the other children at all. His teacher noticed that and suggested that I take him to an organization called Child Find. I know it might sound odd to some that the dean would call me right in the middle of the day when there really hadn't been an incident, but that's just the way school administrators choose to notify parents if there's an issue.

I called Child Find immediately—but the organization had just closed for the day. Later that evening, I broke down in tears as I told Keri what happened. He tried to console me, and though he wore his usual calm facial expression, I could tell that he was just as upset as I was. I don't think either one of us slept a full hour that night. I was too overcome with emotion and fear about what could be wrong with my son. A couple weeks later, I took Diezel straight to Child Find and had him tested. And tested. And tested. After three weeks of enduring every diagnostic evaluation imaginable, I finally received this diagnosis: "Your son is autistic."

My first reaction might shock you—I was furious. For more than two years before that diagnosis, I had noticed that Diezel wasn't developing in the same way that his brother had. We all know that you should never compare children, but the signs were undeniable. For example, Diezel made almost no eye contact; at fourteen months, he stopped making noises altogether—no babbling or baby talk, and no short nouns like *cup* or *juice* or *ball*. He also became very standoffish—he seldom played or socialized with other children. I mentioned all these signs to his pediatrician, and he checked Diezel's hearing—twice. Both tests showed that my son's hearing was completely normal. All kinds of specialists were brought in, but everyone kept saying he was fine. One doctor said, "Oh, he's just a little delayed—don't worry about it." But my mother's instinct told me that something just wasn't quite right. So the fact that I'd been dismissed by so many doctors—only to discover that my son was autistic—made me very angry. A mother always knows when something is wrong with her child.

There have been so many debates about whether vaccines have caused an explosion in the number of autism cases. The drug companies insist that no findings link immunization and autism. Perhaps there isn't a link. Maybe it's just a coincidence that after my son's first MMR vaccine, I began to notice changes in him. He wasn't the same spirited infant I'd brought home with me from the hospital. He seemed distant. He didn't respond to affection. Most children embrace attention from their parents or grandparents. Diezel didn't. At first, I thought it was a personality thing. *He'll probably grow up to be a man who doesn't want company—a loner,* I thought. It's okay to come to that conclusion when your son is a teenager—but not when he's still a toddler.

My initial rage was quickly followed by another strong emotion: guilt. *Is God punishing me for that abortion?* That's the question that ran through my head the moment I heard the diagnosis. Autism wasn't being discussed as much back then as it is now—and because I knew so little about it, I imagined the worst. I also started to go back through my mental files to see if I could connect Diezel's autism with anything I'd done. I know it might sound outlandish to some people, but I actually blamed myself. I knew I'd taken a life—so I believed that God's payback was to give my son autism.

On the day I received the news, I went to the Flamingo to do my show that evening. My heart was so heavy that it felt like it was about to fall right out of my chest. I tried to do my usual warm-up—I'd often go out and say something to the audience, like "A funny thing happened to me on my way over here. I'd just gotten back from Mexico where there was a terrible hurricane, and my son asked me, 'Mommy, did you go through the New Mexico or the old one?' " That's the kind of lighthearted story I'd typically share. But on this night, something far more private and sensitive came spilling out. "I just found out my son has autism," I said with tears filling my lower eyelids. A hush fell over the room. "I heard that right before this show." I wasn't so much feeling sorry for myself as I was lost about what to do next. I didn't even know how to begin helping Diezel.

I got one answer the next afternoon. Overnight, word of my breakdown had already made its way to the press, and like an angel, Suzanne Wright—the cofounder of an advocacy organization called Autism Speaks—called me up directly. "This is not your fault," she told me after revealing that her own grandson has autism. "It's not your son's fault either. There's nothing wrong with our babies—they just learn differently. You just have to figure out the right programs to get him the help that he needs." God sent Suzanne my way at exactly the right moment. During one of the most confusing and painful experiences I've ever survived, she assured me that I wasn't alone—and that my beloved Diezel would be just fine. And in the following years, I would do everything in my power to ensure that he would.

I have sometimes wondered whether God was punishing me for the abortion I had years ago by allowing my son to have autism. Or by giving me so many health issues. Or by having my parents go through such a painful divorce. I know God had nothing to do with those situations. But here's one thing I do know: My view of God as a chastising tyrant rather than as a compassionate father was formed long before I lived through any of these heartaches. If something bad is happening in my life, my knee-jerk response is to believe that I must have done something bad to cause it. Day by day, one thought at a time, I'm working to replace that view with another—that as mysterious as God's ways are to me, I have to believe that He's much more of a healer than a judge.

As much as I don't understand religion, I do often feel God's presence. I know He exists. I know He loves me. I have no doubt that He has sustained me through some of the most difficult circumstances of my life. And once I take God out of the confines of the strict religion box I first learned to put Him in, I can see His care manifested in a hundred small ways. It shows up in the form of my children's laughter. Or on a day when my body feels good and my energy level is a little higher than usual. Or in a simple act of kindness extended to me by a stranger. I don't go to church very often—but for me, God isn't in those four walls, and sometimes just being back in a sanctuary makes me feel as condemned as I did as a girl. Yet I don't need to sit in a church to experience the best of who God is—a comforter, a teacher, a protector, a friend.

TOWARD THE END of 2006, I got a call from a successful entertainer—to protect her privacy, I'm not going to share her name. I'd been telling her just how desperate I was to leave

Blackground. "You have to get away from Barry," she told me. "It's your life—you need to take it back." By that time, I was so tired of fighting with Barry.

Not long after that conversation, I got another call—this one was from my fairy godbrother. "How you doin', Toni Braxton?" he said.

"Well," I said, "life is challenging right now."

Prince promised to help me, and he kept his word: Later that week, Prince had someone from his team call me with the names of a few attorneys. Now you can see why I'll always love Prince—he's the one entertainer who has always reached out to me when I'm down. In fact, once when he was on tour himself, he had his team call me up and ask me if I wanted to be his opening act. The timing and details didn't work out in the case—but I thought it was very sweet of him to look out for ways to help me out. I will always love him.

I didn't even put myself through the trauma of telling Barry that I was planning to leave his label. Instead, I hired an attorney and went straight into litigation. On January 12, 2007, in the U.S. District Court in Manhattan, I filed a lawsuit for $10 million against Blackground. In the suit, I gave the details of how Barry failed to live up to the standards of a good manager. Barry hired his own lawyers to gear up for a fight, and as the back-and-forth between our two camps began, I could see that we were in for a long, painful, and expensive legal battle. Once I sued, Barry eventually countersued to dispute my claim that he had been dishonest with me as a way to lure me away from Arista. In his suit, he claimed that I was dropped from Arista because of poor record sales. Although we disagreed I was so ready to just move on with my life and break free from Barry. That's why I chose to settle out of court.

I was finally positioned to get my career back on track.

CHAPTER 18

The Vegas Showstopper

"Why are you always working so much?" my mother would often fuss. "Six weeks after your last C-section, you were back at work. Keri is very talented—so what is his contribution?" I silently had the same question—and it was starting to cause the kind of resentment that can weigh down a marriage. Toward the end of 2007, I took a two-week vacation from my Vegas show because I was feeling so physically and emotionally exhausted. I knew then that I needed Keri to become a stronger financial contributor. "We've gotta figure something else out because I don't know if I can keep doing these shows," I told Keri. "Let's come up with a plan. I am tired of working this hard."

Don't get me wrong: I believe that Keri wanted to earn

more money for our family, and he has always been a hard worker. But from his perspective, working for me didn't leave him with enough time to pursue other income. I understood his point—which is why I suggested that he stop overseeing my sound production and instead take on other projects. "Maybe you should compliment him more," my mother suggested. "That'll show him how much you appreciate him. Sometimes men need a push." I already felt like I was doing that—but I tried to do it even more.

In the middle of all this, Keri and I were doing our best to make sure Diezel received the highest-quality care—and he was making great progress. We got him several types of intense therapy: occupational therapy, applied behavior analysis (ABA), and speech. Deciding on all his programs and juggling the hours of weekly therapies often creates a wedge between the parents of autistic children. Keri and I were no exception. We never really talked about how stressful it all was (in our relationship, neither of us was great at communicating) so I think we stashed away our feelings and kept moving.

I dealt with my anxiety by staying in survival mode. I just worked. And worked. And worked. Until the day in April 2008 when I started feeling absolutely miserable. "My whole body feels so weak," I told Keri. I think he believed I was becoming a hypochondriac, because something always seemed to be wrong with me. I'd been back and forth to the doctors, and no one could figure out exactly what was causing my fatigue; they knew I was anemic—my hemoglobin was so low that I'd started going in for iron transfusions every Monday.

At times when I was onstage, my heart would suddenly start beating so fast that it felt like it would fall right out of my chest—but then a few moments later, it would go away. When I'd go to the doctors, the tests wouldn't turn up any new issues. *Maybe I just need to laugh,* I thought. *That's always the best medicine.* So I went to see Wanda Sykes, who is one of my favorite female comedians. She did crack me up—but afterward, I still couldn't get it together.

In the next two days, I became even more fatigued. But I wanted to spend some time with the boys, so we gathered around our television upstairs to watch Jerry Seinfeld's *Bee Movie.* Halfway through the film, I felt a pressure in my chest— as if I was trying to walk forward while a three-hundred- pound football player was pushing me back. I made my way down the stairs, one slow step at a time, and I checked my blood pressure using an at-home monitor. It was high as hell— 180 over 118. I chewed a couple of Tums (I thought my chest pain could be indigestion) and walked back up the stairs—but I was so frail that I had to stop and curl up right there at the top of the limestone staircase. "Keri," I whispered, "I have to go to the hospital right now." He rushed over, scooped me up, left the boys with the nanny, and sped off.

The hospital was only two miles away—but it felt like two million. "You're going to have to run these red lights," I whispered to Keri. He shifted into high gear and flew through the next five intersections. Soon after, we pulled up to the front entrance of the ER and Keri helped me out of the car. As he went to park, I practically crawled my way through the glass doors. Do you remember how slowly Mr. Tudball from *The Carol Burnett Show* used to walk? Well, that's how slowly I was walking.

"May I help you?" a receptionist brusquely asked when he spotted me just inside the front door. I could barely talk because I was so out of breath, which is why I whispered something inaudible. "Is it your throat?" he asked, pressing me.

"There's an elephant sitting on me right now," I finally managed to say loudly enough for him to hear. I placed my palm over my chest.

Seconds later, a nurse put me in a wheelchair and rushed me off to an exam room. She checked my blood pressure, gave me some baby aspirin, and drew my blood. Soon after, the doctor came in. "Your troponin levels are elevated," he said. "That could be the sign of a heart attack." They later did an EKG, an echocardiogram, an MRI—the works. "Your blood work reads like you've had a heart attack—but your EKG doesn't," the doctor said. "I'm going to keep you in the hospital for a couple days to do more tests and to monitor you."

During my stay, a male nurse came in for what I thought was a routine check—but he instead had a question for me. "Someone from the *Enquirer* wants to talk to you," he whispered. "Can you do an interview?" I stared at him in silence. I was on so much Ativan that I was barely even conscious—but I was awake enough to know that he was crossing the line. Apparently, someone from the *Enquirer* had agreed to pay this nurse if he could get me to talk. I immediately asked to be released from that hospital against the doctors' orders. After

I signed a slew of paperwork, I then left through a back entrance so I could avoid the paparazzi.

My sister Tamar and her fiancé, Vince Herbert, who is a record company executive, came to see me. At the time, the two were planning their fall wedding, and they stopped by my place to check on me. My mother also flew in. "You don't look good, T," Tamar said. Vince called his friend Mel at Interscope Records; Mel recommended that I see Dr. Shapira, a specialist in Los Angeles. I agreed—but I thought we could all just take the short drive from Vegas over to L.A. "You need to fly, T," Vince said insistently. "You're too sick to make the drive." So Keri packed my suitcase, and my mother stayed with the boys. When we got to the airport check-in, the security people didn't even want to let me onto the flight because I looked so ill. That's just how much of a mess I was. Keri had to call and get clearance from my doctor; a fax was sent to airport officials, and they confirmed that I was indeed on my way to see a specialist. The airport officials reluctantly let me onto the flight.

When Dr. Shapira evaluated me, he said, "I can't even believe they released you from the last hospital." He'd only been planning to run some tests and then release me, but when he saw that my blood pressure was super high (200 over 122), he immediately admitted me to Cedars-Sinai Medical Center. When Dr. Shapira noticed in my records that I'd previously seen Dr. Wallace, a rheumatologist in Los Angeles, he asked me why. "Because my white blood cell count was low," I explained. So at that point, he decided to bring in Dr. Wallace to run some more tests on me, and one seemed to show that I had some kind of heart blockage. That's why Dr. Wallace seemed to think I needed a heart transplant. "You have microvascular angina," he told me. That news made me so hysterical that I had to be given an antianxiety medication. But after both of the doctors did some additional testing, they eventually ruled out the heart transplant and began considering other possibilities for what may be causing my condition.

Two weeks later, Dr. Shapira and Dr. Wallace gave me their conclusion: "You have lupus—and it's the kind that attacks your organs—and yours is attacking your heart." What looked like a heart condition was really just a sign that my body was in a lupus flare-up. When I heard this, I was far more relieved than I was scared. At last, I had an answer.

My diagnosis that day marked the beginning of my road to recovery—but it was also the end of my Vegas run. "You cannot do your show," my doctor told me as he released me from the hospital. "That's way too much singing and dancing around for five nights a week." So between April and August 2008—the month that would've marked the completion of my contract with the Flamingo—I didn't perform. All remaining shows were canceled and my room went dark.

LUPUS IS A tough disease—and I chose not to reveal my diagnosis to the world right away. "If you tell people you have lupus," my managers warned me, "you may not get work." If people perceived me as too weak to work, I could have trouble getting record deals and acting roles. So right after the diagnosis, I kept my news to myself. Keri knew, of course, and so did my mother. But I waited awhile before I told everyone else. It was bad enough that they'd heard I'd had a heart scare; they didn't also need to know that scare had turned out to be a life-threatening disorder.

Once the doctors sent me home with a gazillion meds, I did a lot of my own research on my condition. Systemic lupus erythematosus (SLE is usually referred to as "lupus") is a chronic autoimmune disorder that can affect any organ in the body. The immune system, which normally protects the body, forms antibodies that attack everything from the skin and the lungs to the joints, the kidneys, and even the brain. In my case, lupus affects my organs, and mostly my heart. One of the reasons lupus can be so hard to diagnose is because it often shows up in so many different forms—butterfly-like skin rashes, sore joints, renal failure, blood clots, angina, and chest pains, and even the kind of prolonged and unexplainable exhaustion I'd been experiencing for years. The condition is most common in females—and African-Americans, Asians, and Native Americans are particularly susceptible. More than 1.5 million Americans have the condition. Lupus has no known cure.

My doctors believe that I may have had lupus as far back as my early twenties—and with each passing year, as I pushed myself to work longer and harder, my body became weaker. One of my uncles once lost his life to lupus—but because his lupus was medically induced, I never connected it to the symptoms I'd been having. Researchers still don't know what causes lupus—and though they suspect that there could be a genetic predisposition, there's no scientific proof of that. But here's one thing they are certain about: Stress makes lupus worse. A big part of managing my lupus involves managing my pace and workload.

My diagnosis further strained my relationship with Keri. Once I got out of the hospital, I again struck up the conversation—the one about his financial contribution. I wanted a real break. Keri did make an effort (for a time, he got into the real estate business, and after he made a sale, he once even paid my band's salary for a week, which I thought was very kind of him). He also did some photography work for a short time. But the amount of money Keri could consistently contribute didn't cover our family's expenses.

So I found some other ways to bring in money. That August, despite my doctor's misgivings, I agreed to do the seventh season of *Dancing with the Stars*. Then in October, I signed on with Atlantic Records to start on yet another album—my manager then, Randy Philips, thought that was a good idea. I had a couple possibilities on the table, but I went with Atlantic because I liked the CEO's energy. In addition to needing income, I also wanted to squash some rumors that had surfaced. After I was admitted to the hospital, the whispers began that I was too sick to work—and I knew I had to get in front of that story.

So just before I took the dance floor with my Russian partner, Alec Mazo, I announced to the world that I had microvascular angina. What I didn't reveal is that my heart condition was connected to lupus, because the last thing I needed was for my new record company to lose confidence that I could deliver. That's why I put on my dancing shoes and plastered on a smile—I wanted to make everyone believe that I was feeling just fine. I also had something to prove to myself: Even with lupus, I could live a full and fearless life.

My rehearsals with Alec were between six and eight hours long every day. I pushed myself above and beyond. I brought along a nurse in case anything went wrong (I pretended she was my assistant), and she monitored my blood pressure during breaks. The doctor had put me on an anti-inflammatory drug called Relafen, which sometimes makes the mind go blank. I didn't tell Alec I had lupus, but I did ask him to show me a few basic moves I could do if I ever got stuck. All things considered, I did fine. There were a couple mornings when I struggled to get out of bed because our practice sessions were so strenuous—but I bet a lot of the other dancers felt that way, too.

Alec was an amazing dancer, but we didn't always see eye to eye. He's an atheist—and because I was feeling so emotionally raw at the time, it didn't really help for me to spend most of my days around a person who didn't believe in God's existence. If I mentioned that I was about to say a prayer, for instance, he'd reply with a line like, "I don't believe in prayer." In the midst of everything I was going through, I was trying to reconnect with my spirituality—and Alec wasn't someone who could help me do that.

Even still, I enjoyed the daily workouts (I lost eight pounds!) as well as our live performances. From my first cha-cha-cha to my last West Coast swing, it was a lot of fun to be out on the floor. And to be honest, I was actually disappointed when I got voted off in the fifth week of the show—it kinda broke my heart. But the feeling was short-lived, because I accomplished what I'd set out to do: I waltzed right through my fear and danced myself back to life.

Even before the world knew I had lupus, I discovered that there's just one way to conquer it—one deep breath at a time. Even today, that's my strategy. I have those moments when I'm feeling like the old me—energetic, exuberant, and ready to tackle my to-do list. I also have those moments when I'm feeling wiped out and a little disoriented. Yet each day, I wake up with an incentive that's far more valuable to me than anything else: I want to be here as long as I can. For my family. For my loved ones. For myself.

CHAPTER 19

"How Did I Get Here Again?"

Keri and I separated. By the time we officially announced that excruciating choice to the world in November 2009, we'd already made a private agreement: We would do everything we could to keep our sons' lives normal. When two adults decide that their romance is over, that's certainly painful—but for the children involved, that choice can bring emotional devastation. Keri and I care deeply for our boys—so we made a promise that even after we split, we'd always put their needs ahead of our own.

As far as separations go, ours was pretty amicable. It wasn't that we didn't love each other anymore. Keri has always been my best friend. But some of the issues between us just put too much of a burden on our marriage. We found ourselves disagreeing more than we ever had, and our passion and connection leaked away a little at a time. Marriage is challenging—but when you also work with the person you're married to, it can be an even bigger struggle. Just before Keri moved out, the two of us sat down with our boys. "Mommy and Daddy are going to separate," we told them, "but you'll still get to see both of us as much as you want."

We've lived by our promise to coparent. Even after we first separated in Atlanta, we stayed in the same house for a while. We now each have our own places in Los Angeles, and our kids spend time at both homes. Keri takes Diezel to school, then picks up Denim at the end of the day; after school, Keri and Denim often shoot some hoops. Once homework is done, the three will sometimes wrestle around on the floor, either at my place or at Keri's home, which is close by. When I'm out of town for work, the boys stay with their father. Keri and I have also agreed that we'll always take our sons on a vacation every year—with just the four of us. At some point down the line, if either Keri or I have a significant other in the picture, we'll have to figure out how to take that into account. We just think it's fair to give our kids the experience of having both their parents available. They didn't choose to separate us—we did.

As Keri and I brought our marriage to a tearful finish, I threw myself into my next album. When I'd arrived at Atlantic, Craig Kallman, the CEO, had first said he wanted me to do pop. But then the directors in A&R thought they should

ad-
the

that
hos-
rced
nce I
mpa-
when
anies
com-

taken
event
d that
s con-
cover
t, they
ok for

to

ultry songs that I first became known for.
hat no one was quite sure how to pack-
ually decided on a pathway right down
t by appealing to my core audience with
xton tracks, then we'd cross over to pop.
ut including a collaboration, which is
Songz. After several months in the stu-
than thirty tracks—and we narrowed
November 2009, my duet with Trey
the airwaves. But when we discovered
er tracks were leaked over the Internet
e planned collaborations), we pushed
ease date by a few months. That gave
the studio and create more music.
album—finally came out on May 4,

one of my heart scares, I met an elderly
cardiac rehab. "What are you doing
le. "You're so young." I told her about
"You know what?" she told me. "I've
ks. *Four.* You can't be afraid. You can't
rns out, that woman had just arrived back
ation with her boyfriend—a forty-year-old
don't know that woman's name, and I may
n, but she gave me something important that
doctors had told me that I'd never be able
n, and her conversation was like a heartbeat,
ought me back to life. So I named my album

Pulse as a reminder of that hope. It was also the sign of a gr
ual comeback: The album debuted in the ninth spot on
Billboard 200 chart. *Exhale.*

JUST AS *PULSE* was gathering steam, an issue arose
shifted the headlines—I was being sued. Back when I was
pitalized in Vegas and then confined to bed rest, I was fo
to cancel the remainder of my shows at the Flamingo. Si
was the show's producer, that meant I'd had to hire co
nies to provide services like lighting and flooring. But
my show was cut short, I could no longer pay those comp
the full amount we'd contracted for—so one by one, each
pany served me with a lawsuit.

At first, I thought I was on firm financial ground: I'd
out a liability insurance policy that included coverage fo
cancellation. But when the insurer eventually discovere
the underwriter hadn't specifically listed my pericarditi
dition in the policy, the insurance company declined to
the expenses related to my show's cancellation. In shor
got off on a technicality—and I was suddenly on the h
millions.

Over several months, I tried everything I could
gotiate some kind of settlement with my creditors. I u
of my earnings from *Dancing with the Stars* to hire
who could work out a deal on my behalf. We fought
fought—but in the end, it didn't make much of a diffe
still had debts totaling in the millions and no way to p

off. If I wanted to keep providing for my boys, I knew what I had to do. On September 30, 2010, in a Los Angeles court, I filed for Chapter 7 bankruptcy. Again.

Going broke is one thing—but doing so twice in front of the whole world makes the humiliation practically unbearable. I'll be honest with you: When I filed for the second time, I felt dumb and dumber. It was as if I could hear the whole world shouting in unison, "We told you so!" I'd tried so hard to repair the damage from my first bankruptcy—only to find myself back in the same situation. After the 1998 filing, I couldn't stop crying—but the second time around, my tears showed up in the form of fury. Even though I had no control over getting a heart condition or lupus, I was still so angry. A single question kept reeling through my head: *How did I get here again?*

I became very sick—in part, that's how I got here again. To those who see my second bankruptcy as confirmation that I'm indeed a reckless spender, I understand why it appears that way. That isn't the truth—but trying to convince anyone of that just sounds like the second verse of another sad love song. So I'll simply say this: I hate that it happened. I always will. I'm human, so even now, I'm working through the emotional fallout. But rather than wasting a lot of energy on regret or browbeating myself about the situation, I have chosen to look ahead. In fact, that's really what my entire story is about—falling down, getting back up, learning from my missteps, and then moving forward. I'm still here. Still standing. Still breathing. And that means that I've been given the same gift that we all received when we woke up this morning—the opportunity to start fresh.

Just as they'd done the first time around, the bankruptcy assessors took stock of my belongings. By choice, I wasn't home the day they came to my house in Atlanta: I stayed at my mom's house while my sister Towanda managed everything. Later, she told me the assessor said, "I hate to come and do this, because there are others who have filed bankruptcy who aren't having to go through this—so let's just get it over with." That's one reason I believe that the point was to make an example out of me. After rifling through my possessions, they took all of my jewelry (including my wedding bands).

In some ways, the second bankruptcy was more financially devastating than the first. Don't get me wrong: Even before it hit, things were already tight, because I'd been moving around money to pay off all those creditors (and watching my checking account dwindle down by the day). And on top of that, I had medical bills (although thankfully, I had great health insurance coverage). But here's what made the second time around so hard: I lost my home in Vegas. The whole country was in a housing crisis, so the banks wouldn't work with me to keep the mortgage in place. So we moved to the house I still owned in Atlanta, the one I'd already been trying to sell. I was able to work out a deal to stay in that house, but the bank eventually foreclosed on that home as well—which is why I moved back to Los Angeles and moved into a rented home. In addition to that stress, I'd also taken out a personal loan for millions to launch the Vegas show—but because I'd become so ill, I couldn't repay that loan. And through all of this, I still had a child with special needs—which can potentially cost thousands per year. I didn't have nearly enough money to cover my expenses. That's why I started hustling up tour dates overseas—I did some corporate gigs in Russia, which pays very well (my body wasn't ready to do a full tour). That gave me enough money just to maintain a basic existence.

As fall gave way to winter and 2010 stretched to a close, I decided it was time to begin a new chapter in one particular area of my life—my health. In the months after I was diagnosed with lupus, I'd gotten caught up in the notion that it was best to hide my condition. I really believed that if others knew I had lupus, they wouldn't hire me or even want to be associated with me. But carrying such a big secret is a form of bondage—and above all else, I want to be free.

I'm not a victim of lupus—I'm an overcomer. With each passing day, I'm learning more and more about how to best manage my symptoms so that I can show up as a full participant in my life. Why should I allow what others might say to keep me from declaring that victory? I shouldn't. So just before Thanksgiving, I attended an awards luncheon hosted by Lupus L.A.—an organization I've teamed up with to spread the word about a condition people know too little about. That afternoon, I walked up to the podium with one message: "I am a lupus survivor." Five simple words. One powerful anchor. No more hiding.

CHAPTER 20

Braxton Family Values

I never wanted to do a reality show. Ever. I didn't have some secret dream to see "reality show star" after my name. So several years ago when my sister Tamar first approached me about the idea of creating a docudrama with our family at the center, my answer was very clear: absolutely not. But Tamar persisted. In 2011, she finally uttered the sentence that she knew would press my button: "We all helped you get your start in the music business—now you need to do this for your sisters." I caved.

It's no coincidence that Tamar is the one who approached me with the idea—she has always wanted to be famous. Even back when she was five or six, she used to dress up and pretend she was directing a choir. By the time she was twelve or thirteen, I knew she really wanted it—she'd ask me a thousand questions, and she was curious about every aspect of the record business. We could all see that she wanted it so badly (she had a drive and excitement that I recognized . . .), so I did everything I could to teach her about the industry. Tamar's passion is what led her to keep pressing me to do a show—and that passion, coupled with her personality, made her destined to become such a star on the WE tv series. Our show premiered on April 12, 2011—and there hasn't been a quiet moment since.

People often ask me if our "reality" show is real. It is—at least 99 percent of the time. While we're taping, the producers follow us around with cameras and pick up on what's actually happening in our lives—and believe me, we give them a lot of juicy material to choose from because our lives are so full. The "show" part of our reality show is the other 1 percent: The producers sometimes set up a scene that they can predict will make waves (like in season one, when we surprised Trina with a family intervention about her drinking . . . and yes, Dr. Sherry is actually our family's therapist). Or the producer might ask us to reenact a scenario that has already happened. Let's say, for instance, that Tamar and Trina get into an argument—and I mean a real one, because we never fake arguments for the show. Well, the next time we sisters get together on camera, the producers may tell us to talk about the argument. We don't air everything that happens, of course—certain private family business should always stay private. But all in all, our reality show is very authentic—in fact, there have been times when I wished it was a little *less* real. Let me explain.

In the first season, my sisters, Mommy, and I gathered for a family dinner at a Mexican restaurant. Our father showed up—and it was the first time he and my mother had seen each other since my wedding. "Hello, Miss E," Dad said to Mom. "Hi," she said with zero emotion. Just by the way they greeted each other, I knew it wasn't going to go well. I was right: By the end of the dinner, my father had called my mother a "dirty liar" (which is ironic, since Daddy is the one who cheated with his mistress for ten years . . .) and my mother had accused my father of philandering all around town ("You know that you lay it low and you spread it wide!" she yelled while waving her butter knife). As far as reality TV goes, I don't think it can get much more real—or painful.

Like that scene, dozens of other unscripted, unrehearsed moments have popped up—like that episode when Traci blew her top. During the third season, we'd all encouraged Mommy to go out on a few blind dates . . . we all thought it was time for her to get back out there again. On one of those blind dates, she met a gentleman by the name of Darryl—and she wanted us to meet him. So four of us sisters gathered at a luncheon so we could check him out (Tamar, who was pregnant at the time, stayed home to rest). Right in the middle of our lunch, Traci lashed out at Mommy. As it turns out, her attitude had nothing to do with Darryl—she was pissed because a few days earlier, Mommy had told her to mind her business. But rather than taking that up with Mommy privately, she used our gathering as her moment to go off. Mommy was so embarrassed that she asked Darryl if he could give us a few minutes alone. Here's what you didn't see on the air: In the middle of the scene, the producers actually had to yell, "Cut!" because Traci became so explosive . . . and even after a break, she still didn't cool off. In fact, she stormed out before our lunch was over. Later, the truth behind Traci's temper came to the surface—her husband had been having an affair.

The reality show business is all about creating drama—and that is exactly what it has done in our family. Don't get me wrong: We've always fought—and within a few days after a disagreement, we've always come back around to speak again. But since we began filming *Braxton Family Values,* the periods of silence between the arguing and the making up are becoming longer. The show has brought issues to the surface that are hard to talk about and even harder to heal. That's why I have one big regret about doing the show: It has often pushed us farther away from each other rather than drawing us closer together. But we do get through it okay—the Braxtons always come together in the end.

It's not all bickering and tears—we joke around a lot, both on the set and off. First of all, we've introduced the world to the Braxton family vocabulary, including *scrumdittiliumtious* (Trina's term to describe a yummy-looking man), *cheaterization* (a lifestyle of infidelity), *Secret Squirrel* (our nickname for Towanda, who may know other people's business but will never spill it . . .), and *point, blank, period* (Tamar's way of explaining that the truth has come out . . . and she has nothing more to say). And of course, Tamar made the phrase "dot com" relevant again by adding it to any random subject she was discussing. We also tease each other mercilessly—and to be honest, I hated that when I was a kid. Why? Because what's meant to be funny can often feel cutting. I learned to laugh and just roll with it, but out of all of us, I think Trina has been the most affected by the teasing—I can tell that it hurts her feelings sometimes. Towanda feels it, too, but she covers it well. That doesn't make Tamar hold back with her jokes or opinions—she never had to. My parents (and truthfully, me, too) have always given Tamar lots of leeway, especially as the youngest of the family. If any of us upset Tamar, for example, Mommy and Daddy would often say, "Go apologize to your sister." It was like, "You done upset the baby." That pattern continues today.

Many who watch the show love Tamar—and for good reason. She's feisty, she's fun, and she's super-talented. In fact, I've always thought her voice was special—she has an amazing vocal range. Some have speculated that Tamar and I have a big rift or a secret jealousy between us. Totally untrue. But here's what is true: Like all families, we have differences—and yes, sometimes Tamar's mouth can get on my nerves. At moments I felt there was a competitive nature to our relationship, but despite what people say, I understand how important it is for a younger sister to stand on her own. I will always love her and all of my sisters. And by the way, if anyone thinks Tamar is just exaggerating on the show, let me clear it up for you: The Tamar you see on camera is the same Tamar that my family has been living with since the day she was born. She's not acting. She's just being herself—point, blank, period—which is exactly the way she would put it.

In June 2013, Tamar and Vince welcomed their son, Logan, into the world. All of us gathered in Atlanta for the birth—we were pretty excited about the newest addition to the Braxton family. When he came out, he was all pink and so cute! His light complexion, which he probably got from Tamar, has since darkened up a bit—he's more my shade now. We call him "Logie."

I think Logan is the best thing that ever happened to Tamar—the "baby" now has a baby. She'll be forced to see life different. For instance, Tamar and Towanda once got into it because Tamar was upset that Towanda had to leave a gathering early because she needed to make it to her son's birthday party. Now that Tamar has a child, I'm sure she's getting a better idea of how your priorities change when you become a mom. I've already seen a shift in her: When we all get together, she now seems eager to get back home to the baby. She's also trying to balance her career with having a new son. Tamar is very career-driven—and now, if the baby has a cold or something, he can't travel with her and she feels torn between work and being there for her son as a mom. That's a feeling that I and some of the other sisters can relate to—and now, Tamar gets it, too.

Yes, *Braxton Family Values* is a form of entertainment—but of course, even when the cameras aren't rolling, the "reality" part of the show is actually very true to life. During the third season, for instance, Mommy really was dating a man who appeared in the show. When she finally told us she was getting married to him, I knew he wasn't The One for her—he seemed like a very nice guy, but I could just tell they weren't the greatest fit. But of course, my sisters and I wanted to support her (we were all going to be her bridesmaids), so we began helping her plan the wedding. And to be honest, I was a little excited that my mother had found someone she could share her life with. It quickly became apparent, however, that Mom herself wasn't feeling it. We'd be like, "What are your colors? How do you want your cake? What's your dress?" She didn't have many answers. Once we finally picked a dress and were about to settle on a location, it suddenly became clear that my instincts had been right: She called the whole thing off. That relationship and (near) exchange of vows actually happened—it wasn't just something we made up for the sake of improving our ratings.

So for the most part, the way things seem on the screen is the way they really are. We're ourselves, but we've been edited a bit for TV—which means you don't get to see every aspect of who we are. For instance, here's one thing viewers don't know about Trina: She is very book-smart and always did well in school . . . but we don't have the kind of show where that gets put on display. When we were kids, Trina was the sister who was most likely to be spotted reading. She must've read her share of fairy tales, because even now, she's very Disney. In Trina's view, love will always conquer all. A hopeless romantic—that's who my sister is. That may be one reason that Trina keeps fighting to make her marriage to Gabe work. On the show, Gabe got caught up in infidelity, and Trina took him back. Every woman has a line that cannot be crossed—and for Trina, that line clearly isn't unfaithfulness. But that doesn't mean she wasn't just as hurt as any woman would be. I'm sure it was devastating. In fact, in a later episode, she retaliates by participating in what she called an "oral trans-action." I'm thinking, *Really? You're going to say that on the air?* In retrospect, I think my sister was just angry and trying to get back at Gabe. But in the end, I'm not sure if my sister and Gabe will ever call it quits—that's how much my sister believes in a forever love.

My sister Traci has the biggest heart. She pretends to be tough, but she's actually very sensitive—if you hurt her feel-ings, you may not know it until 10 years later. She's also gen-erous: Even in a moment when she's arguing with you about something, she'll stop and offer you the earrings right out of her ears. "Here, take these," she might say. "They go with your outfit." That's just always the way she's been.

I've always been close with my brother, Mikey. I'm also close with Tamar, yet I'm probably closest with Towanda. The world sees Towanda as The Responsible One—and that is an accurate perception. But there's more to the story: She was the classic middle child in our family—the one who was often struggling to be seen, heard, and recognized. Over the years, I've watched her really break free of that childhood role by standing up for herself and using her voice. I'm really proud of the work she's doing: She has launched a successful business called "The Secret Squirrel," and she trains and places celebrity assistants.

During the time when Towanda worked as my assistant (I so appreciated her help!), she really got a window into my daily world. The financial pressures. The marital challenges. The highs and lows of life in the spotlight. Sharing some of that with Towanda made us tighter—and I realized even more so that I could trust her. I think she finally understood how I came to feel like the Giving Tree of our family—the human version of the local ATM. And now, Towanda is the one sister who also best understands why it's time for me to focus on myself.

The show has also put my own personal life under the spotlight. During one season, I was asked to pose for *Playboy*. As far as I'm concerned, it's an honor to be *asked* at my age—that means someone thinks I still look good enough to pull that off in my forties. I'm still relevant in their eyes. I'd call that flattering—especially since you rarely see a black girl on the magazine's cover! So I actually began considering posing for *Playboy*, and no, that never had anything to do with money. For me, it was like a little smiley face in the midst of all the bull crap with the bankruptcy. As I'm sure you can guess, my family vehemently disagreed. They were like, "Oh my God, you have kids!" In the end, that's what stopped me. I would never do anything that would make Denim and Diezel feel embarrassed. What boy wants to have strangers ogling his mother's boobies?

At another point in the show, I chose to no longer have my brother-in-law as my manager—he'd managed me for a year. It wasn't personal at all—I love Vince and always will. It was simply a business decision I had to make, because mixing family with work is a conflict of interest. I've known Vince since the early days of my career—we met while I was working on my first album, and he was the producer on the song "How Many Ways." We've always been cool, and I really respect him as one of the smartest people in the music business. So long before the cameras started rolling, I let him know that we needed to change directions—I wanted him to hear that for the first time directly from me, not on the set of our reality show. I'm sure he was disappointed by the change—but Vince has never been much of a talker, so we didn't discuss it much beyond that. But since that all happened, we've continued to be close. He's one of the people I can still rely on to lend a listening ear and a wise perspective.

It was on the show that I first really went public with my lupus diagnosis. It was also when viewers started noticing that my face looked puffy on some of the episodes. I'm on a drug called Kenalog, which is a steroid, and every few months I have to get a shot. Ever see me with a moon face even when the rest of my body is skinny? That usually means I've just had a shot. That's one of the side effects of the medication—I get a moon-like face. I actually hate getting them. What girl do you know who wants to be at her best weight, only to look in the mirror and see chubby cheeks? When I was performing on

Dancing with the Stars, I had to get a shot—and even though I'd lost weight from all that dancing, my face was still round and puffy.

Despite my initial misgivings about doing the show, some good has come out of it. For one thing, it has gradually changed my view of my mother. After that major confrontation my parents had during the first season, I started to see just how hurt Mommy was by my dad's infidelity. I already knew she was hurting, of course—but that explosion showed me just how deep the wound was. Yes, my mother is my parent—but above all else, she is a woman. Children always put their parents on a pedestal, and I did the same with mine. But that day, I began to see Mommy for who she really is—a person who carries some of the same hopes and heartaches that we all do. That's why I think my mother was incredibly brave to end her marriage. She met my father when she was fourteen, she married him when she was just seventeen, and she knew no other life outside of him for thirty years. Now that I am a woman myself, I recognize and respect her for showing so much courage.

As for my father, he's always the one in the family that we can talk to—he's easy to have a conversation with. If any of us tells him that we're disappointed about something that happened in our childhood, he is quick to apologize. He doesn't judge. He just listens. My brother Mikey is also a great listener—the men in our family are much better communicators than us women are! Mikey is also quite the prankster: He'll call me up and say, "Do you have change for a penny?"

Doing the series had made my sisters recognizable to millions of viewers—and that's one of the best results I could've hoped for. My biggest sigh of relief will come when they are all ultra-famous superstars. But even if that never happens, I've already made a choice: My job is done. *Braxton Family Values* is the final punctuation mark on a sentence of guilt that has gone on for too many years—since that day in 1991 when my mother, in her anger, told me, "Don't forget your sisters."

At the end of our series' first season, I finally gathered the courage to ask my mother about something that has bothered me for a long time—her rage-filled reaction when I told her I would take the solo deal. Mommy paused and stared at me. "I was just doing what I had to do to keep my family together," she explained. She went on to admit that she wasn't ready for her children to disperse—but rather than resolving her parental fear, she instead handed me the burden of keeping the Braxtons together.

Two decades later, here's what I finally understand: My sisters weren't my responsibility in the first place. Just because someone hands you a weight doesn't mean you have to take it. I know that now—but I didn't at twenty-three. That's why I not only took the burden—I willingly carried it around on my shoulders and allowed it to rob me of some of the most amazing years of my life. I can't get those years back. None of us can return to the past. But there's still one powerful thing I can do—put down the weight. That's exactly what I've done—at last.

CHAPTER 21

Breathing Again

I never meant to retire. But when I appeared on a February 2013 episode of *The Wendy Williams Show,* I told Wendy that I was done with making records. I wish I hadn't opened my mouth—but let me tell you why I did.

First things first: I didn't even go on Wendy's show to talk about my music career. I was actually there to chat about my role in *Twist of Faith,* a Lifetime movie that I'd taken a role in. But once we covered that ground in the interview, I got very comfortable in my chair, mostly because Wendy and I have always been cool. I practically forgot the cameras were there—I'm sure that has something to do with constantly taping *Braxton Family Values.* So when Wendy said, "I heard that you are done recording," my mouth started moving before my brain could catch up—and the following day's head-line became TONI BRAXTON ENDS HER MUSIC CAREER.

I may not have intended to tell Wendy that I was finished—but there was some truth to my statement. For months, I'd been struggling with myself about what to do next in my career—and in my life. My last few records hadn't sold as well as those earlier in my career. My marriage was over. My lupus was becoming more of a challenge to manage. And just the thought of spending hours in the studio made me feel more exhausted than excited. As much of a fighter as I am, I still have those moments . . . those days . . . those weeks when I just don't want to pry myself out of bed and face the world. So when I walked out onto Wendy's set last year, I was carrying all of those emotions with me. And once Wendy gave me her usual "Hey, girl!" treatment, a little of what I'd been feeling just came spilling out as if we were just two friends, catching up one-on-one. It just so happens that the whole world was listening in on our conversation. Oops.

Once the headlines hit, other singers started reaching out. Missy Elliott. Barbra Streisand. And even one of my musical heroes, Anita Baker. They all had the same message: "You cannot retire. I've felt exactly how you're feeling—but it's just not time." Missy even rang me on my cell one afternoon and said, "Hey, whatcha doin', Toni? You should swing by the studio and hang with me." With such an outpouring of support, I suddenly didn't feel so alone. Plenty of other artists had come to the crossroads where I stood—and they had pressed forward.

I'm at a new juncture right now—one that has both everything and nothing to do with music. My marriage has been over for a while, but the actual divorce in the summer of 2013 made our split official. I know it was the best decision for us to separate, but it still makes me sad sometimes. On the day I stood and exchanged vows with Keri, I wanted it to last forever, and I believed that it would. But some things just can't continue—and our romance was one of those things. Even still, Keri and I are both committed to making sure that our sons know how much we love them. We're friends. Long before there was a romance, there was a solid friendship in place, and that foundation will remain. And no matter how our connection evolves in the coming years, Denim and Diezel will always be our priority. We've promised our sons that.

My mom and sisters have nudged me to get back out there and start dating. I've gone out a couple times, but to be honest, I don't think I really know *how* to date. First of all, where am I supposed to meet someone—in the fresh produce section at Whole Foods? And what do I say during all those awkward silences that pop up during dinner? Tamar says I'm a control freak—but I think I just find the whole thing unnerving. In time, I'm sure I'll figure it out, because I do want to have another relationship. And no, I'm not trying to be a cougar—a gentleman in his late forties or fifties would be perfect. And if he's financially comfortable, all the better.

For now, it's me and the boys—and our days are busy with school, homework, and family time. I'm a cooker (I call myself the Barefoot Contessa of my family!), so a couple nights a week, I make dinner for the three of us—like maybe salmon glazed with honey and garlic. "You make the kind of food you'd find in a five-star hotel!" my sisters often say, teasing me. "Nobody wants to eat like that all the time!" But trying out new recipes has always been my thing (I'm addicted to the Cooking Channel). I wish I could put a hot meal on the table every night, the way my mother did when I was growing up, but she was a full-time homemaker. For me, two or three nights a week is plenty—and besides that, Denim, Diezel, and I usually begin our days by having breakfast together.

Both of my sons are great students—and Diezel has made so much social and academic progress that he's now considered high functioning. In fact, if you didn't know he'd ever been diagnosed with autism, you probably wouldn't figure it out. That's because he has been in such intense therapy for so many years—and when it comes to intervention, early diagnosis makes all the difference. He excels in math, but like many autistic children, he has to work harder at reading. Texting on his phone has helped him tremendously. If he misspells a word, the phone automatically corrects it—and that reminds him how to spell it. The first few years after he was diagnosed, he was also surrounded by what autism advocates call "typical peers"—meaning that he was in a school where not everyone was autistic. And did I mention that he's now at a regular private school? I'm one of the lucky parents: my son's early diagnosis and extensive therapy changed everything.

I'm an international spokesperson for Autism Speaks—and Diezel has sometimes been able to join me in that work.

For instance, I got to go to the U.N. in 2011 and share what it is like to mother a child who has autism. Diezel came with me—and he even talked with a correspondent from ABC News in the press room. Everyone was so excited to meet him—but probably not nearly as excited as he was to be there.

Denim says he wants to be a basketball player—or at least that's his Plan A for right now. Plans B and C are attorney and judge. But his plans change all the time. He's a super smart boy—he's a year ahead because he skipped pre-K and went straight to kindergarten. He's also a great big brother to Diezel. A few years back, one of Denim's friends once said, "What's wrong with your brother?" Denim said, "He's autistic—you got a problem with that?" That was one of my proudest mommy moments. It let me know that what I've been teaching my sons about family and sticking together is being applied.

Diezel says he wants to be an actor, and maybe that dream will stick: He made his screen debut in *Twist of Faith*. Neither of my sons wants to sing—and I've never wanted to push my children toward entertainment or any other career path. I understand that my sons don't actually belong to me. They are just gifts that I've been entrusted with for a time. As a mom, my job is to love them, mold them, teach them—and then to release them to live the lives they choose for themselves.

MY SECOND BANKRUPTCY became settled in July 2013. I now have a clean slate—but it did come at a cost. For one thing, I lost the rights to several of my songs, including "You're Makin' Me High" and "How Many Ways" . . . thankfully, I was able to hold on to "Un-Break My Heart." And you want to hear how I discovered I'd lost the rights to more than two dozen songs? This is another example of how nutty things can get in my industry.

True story: Just before I set out on a performance tour, I did an interview with a newspaper reporter. My publicist set up the call, connected us, and then stayed on the line. So the interviewer goes, "I read that you lost the publishing rights to a lot of your songs. So what's next for Toni Braxton?" I paused. "Excuse me?" I finally said. I had no clue what she was talking about. Right then, my publicist cut into our conversation and put the reporter on hold. "We'll call you right back," she told the journalist. A couple minutes later, my manager called me. "We had to auction off your publishing rights," he said. Apparently, my attorneys had gone to the auction to buy back my songs (once the bankruptcy was settled, a buyback was an option) but when someone put in a large bid for the song, my lawyers had decided it wasn't worth it to offer a higher bid. "The song rights will eventually revert back to you anyway," my manager explained. He apologized profusely that he hadn't yet circled back to tell me what happened at the auction. Let me be honest with you: Even though my lawyers' rationale makes sense, I'm nonetheless pissed that I no longer own the rights to those songs. But then again, there's far more to be grateful about in my situation than there is to be annoyed about. I've been given a chance to start over. Twice. And I intend to use the opportunity to move myself and my family to the next place.

IT WAS KENNY—my brother in the music business—who ultimately convinced me not to hang up my microphone. "You're just going through a hard time," he told me. "You're angry about your life. You're angry about some of the choices you made. You've gotta work through that—but you can't let it stop you from recording." That breakthrough conversation turned into a duet album that we called *Love, Marriage, Divorce*.

Working with Kenny again on this new album has been as much fun as I expected—and then some. At this point, we're like family, so the jokes are constantly flowing. We did have to sort out a few issues in the beginning of our collaboration: Because Kenny is the one who first molded me as a musician, I think he has a tendency to see me as his little sister. So during our recording process, I'll admit that I was at first walking on eggshells when it came to expressing my ideas—but that changed rather quickly as I asserted myself and began to speak up. This project is 50-50, so our artistic opinions carry equal weight. I have just as much invested in our success as Kenny does. Also, when I would show up at Kenny's studio for us to work together, the engineers would sometimes say, "Well, we have to wait till Kenny comes in." I'm like, "Guys, I'm here— we can start." We are full partners—and I had to make that known in a nice but firm way. When I'm in the room, my voice matters. My perspective matters. I matter.

"Hurt You"—that's one of the first singles Kenny and I worked on. He wrote the hook, which I must say is pretty darn perfect. But when it came to the verses, I wasn't in love with some of the lyrics and melodies he wrote, so I said, "Let me try some stuff." When I came back the following day with some lyrics, he didn't really like what I'd created. At first, he resisted. But he surprised me a week or so later when circled back and said, "You know, you're right: What you came up with actually works."

In one part of the bridge in "Hurt You," I added the line "loving you causes so much pain." Kenny asked, "What do you mean by that?" I said, "Have you ever been in love with a person, and you try to love him, but no matter what you give him, you can never make him happy—so it makes you feel pain?" He kinda understood—yet he had a different perspective, because he has always been the kind of man who provides for his family. But I was there to remind him that in our world, it's often the working class woman who pays the bills. Guys are becoming the new girls. So there are many men at home with the kids, and plenty of them earn less than women do. "But that's a small percentage of situations," he protested. I said, "Kenny, you live in Bel Air. Once you get out of your neighborhood, there's a greater percentage of people who are in exactly that situation." It was conversations like this one that made our collaboration so rich. You can't put out an album called *Love, Marriage, Divorce* and not represent the experiences of both genders—so we worked hard to be sure that our lyrics would resonate. The only way you can do that is by writing from a place of honesty. And since Kenny and I have both been through painful divorces, we had no shortage of material from which to draw on.

Either Kenny or I wrote pretty much every song on the album. The melody and lyrics came to us through so many different channels. For instance, after my mother initially discovered my dad's affair, she was so angry. The rage was practically written across her forehead. One day when she must've been in a lot of pain, she said something like, "I hope that woman breaks his heart." That's what inspired the song "I Wish." One of the lyrics is, "I hope she breaks your heart like you did me." That turned out to be one of Kenny's favorite songs on the album. He goes, "Not only are you an artist— you're a real songwriter." It felt good to hear Kenny say that.

The whole project with Kenny is a risk for me—a way for me to push myself to try something different. Here's the thing: When you've been in this business for as long as I've been in it, you've gotta constantly find ways to reinvent yourself, to keep learning new things. Otherwise, the challenge is no longer there—and once the challenge disappears, so does the passion, interest, and fun. Of course, I've sung with Kenny before—but I've never done it as his full partner. I've also never done a tour in which I've performed onstage with another singer—that's new territory, and it's an exciting part of this process that I'm looking forward to.

Even before Motown released our album in 2014, I arranged to do a month-long tour of my own across the United
States. I wanted to do a test run: In light of my lupus, would
my health and energy level hold up during a tour that involved
four concerts a week? The answer was a resounding yes. It
felt so good to be back onstage in some of our country's larg-
est arenas, with hundreds of thousands of people gathering
to enjoy music. I sang a lot of my classics, like "Un-break
My Heart" and "Breathe Again," and of course, I also threw
in some newer material. Sometimes I'd yell out to the audience, "What do ya'll want me to sing tonight?" and then go
with whichever song I heard people screaming out. And yes:
Sometimes I would forget a few of the lyrics to my own songs!
Here's the trick every performer knows: When you go brain
dead, just ask the audience to sing along with you—fans often
know the lyrics better than I do!

I had never felt more alive than I did when I was out there
performing on the road for that month—it was like getting
lifted and fortified. I now find it hard to believe that I ever considered retiring. I love what I do way too much to think about
letting it go. Just about everything on the tour went even better than we'd planned—unless, of course, you recall the little
"wardrobe malfunction" I had on the stage while I was in New
Brunswick, New Jersey. In-between songs, I went offstage for
a minute for a quick change—and when I put on my new outfit, a clasp must have been broken. So when I got out there onstage and start singing again, all of a sudden I started feeling a

little breeze on my butt! I finally realized that the back half of my dress was falling off, and even though I had a sheer body suit underneath, it sure did look like my backside was naked back there. Someone in the audience lent me a sports jacket to cover up my buns—and I kept right on singing through the whole ordeal! Life is like that sometimes—you often just have to keep it moving, even when your booty is exposed.

I got to hang with my sisters while I was on the road. Trina and Towanda, who did the background singing, traveled with me. Traci even joined us on some of the tour dates. I arranged for Trina to sing a song in my show, because her single, "Party or Go Home," was out. And during the concert, I also showed little clips from *Braxton Family Values*. And between concerts, my sisters and I would spent a lot of time laughing and catching up with each and sharing meals and drinks. It was so much fun.

I also got to use the tour to engage women on the topic of lupus. L.A. Lupus, the organization for which I serve as a spokesperson, gathered groups of about 10 women at each one of my concert stops. Most of the women had lupus—or they were connected to someone who was living with the condition. In a way, it felt like a group therapy session: We got together backstage for a few minutes and just shared things like how we were feeling that day, what form of lupus we'd been diagnosed with, and what kinds of treatments we'd found to be most effective. I'll never forget a young black woman who showed up with tears on her lower lids during my stop in New

York. "My sister just died of lupus," she revealed to the group. We each offered her words of support and plenty of hugs. And of course, there were stories of hope as well: One woman had been diagnosed with lupus when she was just fourteen—and at age thirty-two, she was still going strong and feeling great. She'd just completed a round of chemo (when lupus is in its advanced stages, chemo is one of the treatments doctors try), and she was thrilled that her hair was finally growing back. "Look—it's even long enough for me to put in a couple of weave tracks!"

That day I sat on Wendy's couch, it wasn't that I'd actually fallen out of love with music. It was that I'd fallen out of balance in my life. I could tell you that I'm now completely centered again. That would be a lie. My journey doesn't come wrapped in a shiny package with a neat little bow placed on top. Life is more messy than that. Circumstances fall apart, then we pull them back together—only to have them come undone another time. I'm starting to realize that we're not supposed to keep everything lined up and in perfect order—even with our best efforts, we can't accomplish that anyway. Instead, we're meant to find lessons in both the chaos and the cleanup.

I'm still trying to figure out everything there is to learn in my life. Some lessons are pretty straightforward: When you hand over the reins of your life to someone else, you render yourself voiceless and powerless. Other lessons are harder to recognize: What is there to learn from getting lupus? Or having a son with autism? Or watching your parents' thirty-year marriage suddenly disintegrate? I don't think I'll ever understand why some things happen. But the point may not be to make sense of the most difficult situations. It could be that we're here to learn how to breathe through them. After a lifetime of holding my breath, that's what I'm finally doing.

ACKNOWLEDGMENTS

So many people have stood by me during my journey. I am deeply grateful to all those who've supported me and offered their love and encouragement. Here are a few people I'd like to thank publicly:

My managers, Craig Baumgarten and Marcus Grant: Thank you not only for overseeing the details of my career, but also for listening, even when I wasn't talking. You're the best! Whatcha Doing? :)

I really should be thanking your wives, too. They put up with the repeated calls, questions, and concerns. Shawn Baumgarten and J'Vaughn Aubry-Grant—I appreciate you!

My literary agent, Steve Fisher: Thank you for handling

the publishing side of my work—I couldn't have become an author without your help.

Mommy and Daddy: You believed in me long before the world knew who I was. It's because of you that I am the entertainer that I am today. I will forever love you . . . both.

Denim and Diezel: I love you both more than you could ever know. You are my favorite show.

My sisters and brother: I wish I could give my kids what we had—lots of each other. We are The Braxtons . . . always!

Trina Braxton: Thank you for reading the book manuscript over and over again and helping me not to be embarrassed.

Towanda Braxton: A very special thanks to you, The Responsible One, for the millions of hours you've spent taking care of me . . . even though you think you don't work for me anymore! :) And thank you, too, for sending your Squirrels.

David Brokaw: I heart u, I heart u, I heart u.

Dr. Sherry Blake: The perfect "listening ear."

Alex Tanjala: I miss you every day!

Ashlee Braxton, Lorenzo "Zo" Williams, and James Philips: I would be up a tree without you.

My fans: for sticking by me, even when it was sticky.

And of course, none of this would've been accomplished without the skills of my team at HarperCollins. Thanks to the captain of my book team, Lisa Sharkey, who signed me up; Amy Bendell, who has worked tirelessly on the manuscript;

and Paige Hazzan, who has spent hours settling the details. Much appreciation and excitement also goes to the art director, photo editor, marketing team, and the extraordinary sales force at HarperCollins. I am very appreciative of your enthusiasm and support.